ENDORSEMENTS

"So, you plunged off into a following-Jesus-anywhere life. And you grew. A lot. But after years, that same sweet voice that drew you toward evangelical faith now seems to pull beyond it. Evangelicalism's exclusions are looking incongruous. Orthodoxy hinders as many as it helps. You want to love.

You're not alone. Thousands hear that call. As Dan Henderson describes his journey, you'll see some of your story. You'll be encouraged. Trust that voice in your heart. Have courage. Find your way. These words may help."

—**Monte Asbury**, Pastor, New Oaks Church of the Nazarene (retired), Washington, Iowa, USA

"Daniel's retracing of his own path will no doubt prompt readers to reflect on their own journeys of religious identity and social awareness. More importantly, it can impel readers, including those of us who find that collective Christian action may be the best way to do so, to reflect on what their values require from us to address the social inequities they see and to make their communities more wholesome places."

—**Monie Hayes, PhD**, College Instructor

"The reformation of ones faith is no mean task. It is more than a mere decision, a cold calculation. It more than a change of mind. It is a journey that takes courage and determination. There is no roadmap or blueprint for this journey. Although some will begin with their head, others with their heart, it is the heart that is the critical organ in this venture. There is no formula. We each must feel our way forward. The path is one to be experienced. Others may help us along the path, but no can show us THE way.

This book chronicles the journey of one in process. It is an individuals, if I may reappropriate the term, testimony. It is told in a way that is intimate, personal and accessible. Honest and not heavy handed. This book, along with others, can be a companion as we seek to untie the knot that was once our faith tradition and weave out of it something more beautiful, more personal and more relevant."

—**Brian May**, former teaching colleague to Daniel Henderson

"Daniel Henderson's *Confessions of a Recovering Evangelical* is a remarkable book. As a 'lapsed Lutheran' who grew increasingly estranged over the years from the Christianity of my youth, it's also a comforting work. At 68 years old, I watched at first with concern, then frustration, and finally with anger at what the "Christian" right hath wrought since the days of Reagan and Falwell that set the stage for Trump, and potentially the destruction of a faith. Henderson lays it all bare in one of the best contemporary histories of faith and politics, covering the past few generations that I have read. It's also a gut-wrenching, honest book that took courage to write.

While having strayed from the church long ago, I still retain a child-like faith, taking comfort daily in the Beatitudes, which the "Christian" right have trampled. In this book, Henderson gives those like me a chance to circle back and consider what we may have lost. He also provides purchase to those who recognize that they have been duped by con men and scoundrels calling themselves Christians and are seeking a way out. Let's hope they take it."

—**Bob Leonard**, PhD, columnist and radio personality, KNIA/KRLS Knoxville/Pella/Indianola, Iowa

Sherri —
Continue the journey —
Dan Henderson

CONFESSIONS OF A RECOVERING EVANGELICAL

OVERCOMING FEAR AND CERTAINTY TO FIND FAITH THROUGH DOUBT AND QUESTIONING

DANIEL HENDERSON

First Edition

Cover design by Rafael Polendo (polendo.net)
Layout by Matthew J. Distefano

ISBN: 978-1-957007-27-4

This volume is printed on acid free paper and meets ANSI Z39.48 standards. Printed in the United States of America

Published by Quoir
Oak Glen, California
www.quoir.com

CONTENTS

FOREWORD

WE'VE BEEN WAITING FOR Daniel Henderson's book, *Confessions of a Recovering Evangelical*. I know I have.

For over twenty years I have written and spoken about the topic of spiritual abuse and Religious Trauma Syndrome. I have a private counseling practice and have trained other counselors and spiritual directors in working with men, women and children who have been victimized by religious toxicity.

In 2019 I founded *The Center for Non-Religious Spirituality* to offer support and resources to those who are seeking healing and restoration from the wounds left behind by an abusive church and toxic religious indoctrination. In conversations about "spiritual abuse" many people think of extreme cases like "cults." But some of the most damaging churches or religious groups can appear culturally relevant, progressive, friendly, and family-oriented on the surface.

It is not novel these days for a book to be written that rails against the absurdities of fundamentalist religion. Much of the writing on toxic religious deconstruction makes fodder of traditional Christian doctrine and exposes the dysfunctional and destructive dynamics of the institutional church. In my view, these offerings often lack the depth of insight to address the deeply rooted wounds of toxic religion that sabotage our relationship with ourselves and life and leave people ill-equipped to sort out the complexities of contemporary Western culture.

A focus of Christian Evangelicalism has always been one's "individual personal relationship with God" and fuels a highly individualistic spirituality. Evangelicalism is about *you* "getting saved" so that *you* are right with God so *you* will go to heaven. It also emphasizes what *you* are going to gain (inner peace, favorable personal circumstances, financial gain) as a result of *you* believing and doing the right things.

As it turns out, much of the focus of religious detox and deconstruction work is also highly individualistic. Yes of course, overcoming spiritual abuse and religious trauma is a matter of an individual person addressing and overcoming their own particular individual wounds, and reconstructing a more authentic, meaningful and liberating individual spirituality. However, there is another critical aspect of this deconstruction and reconstruction journey, which involves our fundamental understanding of the world and how we participate in it.

I appreciate how Martin Luther King, Jr. understood that the self-actualization of the individual is not purely an individualistic matter and has a profound collective dimension to it, which Martin Luther King, Jr. articulated with these words, "Whatever affects one directly, affects all indirectly. I can never be what I ought to be until you are what you ought to be. This is the interrelated structure of reality." French philosopher Simone de Beauvoir wrote, "A free man is one whose end is the liberation of himself and others."

Daniel Henderson's book, *Confessions of a Recovering Evangelical*, is a brilliant roadmap for a deep-dive destruction of the impact of toxic religion. After an accounting of his own exodus out of Evangelical Christianity, Daniel devotes the opening chapters of his book to fleshing out a post-Christian framework for reimagining "faith" and the Bible and addressing life's greatest existential questions such as the existence of God, the purpose and meaning of human existence, as well as death and the afterlife.

But Daniel takes the matter of religious deconstruction into our current cultural milieu, which is the piece I often find lacking or absent altogether. *Confessions of a Recovering Evangelical* distinguishes itself not only as a thoughtful and compelling deconstruction of Christian theology, but how it unravels the impact of toxic religion in shaping people's fundamental orientation toward matters such as social justice, racism, white privilege, environmentalism, sexuality, gender identity, abortion, gun violence, police corruption, Me Too movement, and Trumpism. This is the kind of next-level deconstruction we need in overcoming the deleterious societal impact of Western toxic religion.

For example, Daniel writes about the Black Lives Matter Movement:

> When white Evangelicals throw up their guilt defense, it is really a tactic that goes back to Billy Graham's theology. There is nothing we can do about racism until Jesus returns so why are you talking about it? It is a deflection and diversionary tactic aimed at keeping Evangelicals from feeling guilt or having to take action against racism . . . I am amazed at the reaction of Evangelicals to BLM. They are usually the first ones to counter with the worn-out disrespectful phrase, "All Lives Matter." I know because I reacted the same way. It is almost automatic. Evangelicals think when someone says, "black lives matter," it is supposed to elicit guilt. It's not. The emotion that is being called for is empathy.

About Evangelicalism's rejection of the LGBTQ+ community, Daniel writes:

> Evangelicals are still of the belief by and large, that being gay is a choice that they can choose or not choose. But the first epiphany in my little Evangelical brain was to realize that I did not at any time in my life, ever choose my own sexual orientation or preference. There was never a day where I sat down and reasoned it through and decided, "I think I'll go

> ahead and be attracted to the opposite sex for the rest of my life." It was just there.
>
> I strongly suspect this is the case for those that experience same sex attraction. They have no more chosen that orientation than I did. In fact there were probably a lot of disincentives to choose that sexual preference given the bigotry, discrimination and hostility toward gays. Why would anyone choose that fate? Who wants the abuse?
>
> The intolerance and hostility toward gays that permeates the Evangelical community is not only distasteful but is exactly the opposite of what I read about in the New Testament in the teachings of Jesus. The love of Christ and the inclusiveness of spirituality makes the continued persecution and exclusion of gay people, totally unacceptable.

In my two decades of toxic religion recovery work with people, I have recognized a progression of steps and stages in the process of disentangling oneself from toxic religious beliefs and practices. There are deepening levels of religious deconstruction.

Many people begin by removing themselves from a religious community that they feel is having a detrimental impact on their mental, emotional, psychological well-being and health. Another level of deconstruction involves divesting ourselves from various religious beliefs and practices that we no longer accept.

There is a cause-and-effect nature of toxic religious beliefs. The recovery process involves identifying the deeply rooted toxic beliefs that are the root cause of self-sabotaging dynamics and neuroses that govern our lives such as shame, fear, anxiety, worry, depression, self-flagellation, inauthenticity, suppression, self-rejection, perfectionism, and powerlessness.

It's common for people who leave religion to become a staunch critic of religion. Notice that in both cases, the reference point is still religion. A person can be a religious fundamentalist, but they can also be an anti-religion fundamentalist. One of the great contributions of Daniel Henderson's book is that the endgame is not simply switching sides but reconstructing an entirely new framework and mindset to be liberators in our world.

Confessions of a Recovering Evangelical is not a heady, academic, verbose, pedantic diatribe. It is an unpretentious, heartfelt, humble, brutally honest, hard hitting, captivating, ground-breaking and compassionate work. Daniel is a masterful storyteller. You don't have to arduously slog through the chapters. It's a book you can't put down and enjoy reading. Daniel's depth of insight is drawn from his own life's journey and is shared in the stories of people and experiences that have shaped him. Dan writes with the honesty, humor, and humanity of a Anne Lamott, and the exacting, scrappy, no-nonsense and fiery spirit of a Cornel West.

Daniel's writing sheds light on the fact that the deconstruction of one's religion isn't the end point but only the starting point of reconstructing a whole new vision and perspective on faith. He shows how this deconstruction process has real life implications for politics, social justice and the evolution of our society. The book is usefully divided into five major sections:

- Part I – Deconstructing Faith Through Doubt
- Part II – Faith & Racial Justice – Becoming Anti-Racist
- Part III – Faith & Gay Rights: Love Is Love Regardless
- Part IV – How Evangelical Ideology Threatens Culture
- Part V – Other Deconstruction Heresies

It will especially appeal to people who seek to cultivate a more authentic, human, freethinking, courageous, and socially conscious spirituality.

I often say that Christianity is not the fault of Jesus. There are many ways that Jesus is universally relevant, regardless of one's religious, spiritual or philosophical belief-system. Jesus both affirmed what was good and confronted what was wrong in his own religious tradition. He taught that love is and should be the ultimate fulfillment of all religious teaching. Jesus pointed out the hypocrisy of claiming a close relationship with God while perpetuating discord and hostility in human relationships. He confronted the mentality of judging others, and instead told people to look in the mirror.

Jesus taught human solidarity where every person sees themselves as a "neighbor" to those in need. He extended love, compassion and friendship to all people without condition. He affirmed the inherent and equal worth of all human beings, regardless of their status or place in the world. Jesus confronted systemic oppression and took on institutional power structures that perpetuated it. He did not seek to convert people to any religion or belief-system but challenged his followers to embrace and follow the spirit of love within themselves. Jesus affirmed that every person has the responsibility and authority to build a world of peace and harmony that works for everyone.

Many people who leave church and religion don't necessarily want to abandon all possibilities for God, faith or even Jesus. Daniel Henderson's book *Confessions of a Recovering Evangelical* shows us how to do this and what it might look like individually and collectively. One's religious deconstruction does not have to lead to nihilism, anti-religion fundamentalism, and spiritual deprivation, but can open entirely new vistas for reimagining what it means to be divine and human.

—**Jim Palmer**, Founder, Center for Non-Religious Spirituality, Author, *Inner Anarchy* and *Notes from (Over) the Edge*

DEDICATIONS

In writing about this personal deconstruction journey, I am not trying to change anyone's mind about their faith. Faith is always a personal journey. It is not my goal to get people to leave their church or religion. If you are fully convinced that the Evangelical church meets your needs, and you are happy then this book may not be for you.

However, if you are like tens of thousands of others who have discovered that the Evangelical mindset doesn't answer your questions and doesn't hold up to the scrutiny of doubt then I think you will find a kindred spirit within these pages.

Deciding to leave your religious affiliation of many decades isn't a decision that you make lightly. My journey took many years and is still not finished. I'm not sure it ever will be. But if you are seeking something beyond what the Evangelical faith has become and are looking for something that is inclusive, expansive and allows you to see yourself as more than a rotten, depraved person doomed to hell, then this story may be of comfort.

It is my hope this book will provide you with some comfort along your journey. We are fellow travelers who are looking for something more than a creed, a statement of faith or a set of beliefs by which you can be considered "saved."

If you are seeking an inner kingdom of God where the Christ narrative resonates with your soul, opens your mind and heart to all people, breaks down theological barriers and tribes, then I think you'll find this narrative to be useful.

I do wish to dedicate this book to the thousands of students that I had contact and relationships with during a 30-year career in education. Teaching was my calling and my joy. I would often say to people, "do they really pay me to do this?" I loved teaching students about history and opening their eyes to our past so that they would have a platform to launch into their own futures.

Unfortunately, there were many years when, because of my Evangelical blinders, I restricted their view and understanding of history and human nature by repeating the dogma and ideology of a conservative Christian worldview. For that I am deeply sorry and repentant. I hope that by committing myself now to my own recovery from that distorted world view I can still influence some of those I might have led astray.

If there were "do-overs" I would have been much more adamant about encouraging students to question authority, including mine. Teaching in private religious schools is not an environment where questioning authority is encouraged or rewarded. I should have encouraged students to do more of it.

I also should never have encouraged students to accept blind conformity to a religious ideology that was harmful to them. Of course, I would have been fired very quickly, but in hindsight, I'm sure I could have found subversive ways to encourage such skepticism.

Now, in the twilight of my career, I am even more dedicated to teaching and encouraging skepticism, truth seeking, and questioning, especially of religious doctrine and dogma.

Reject any religious authority that teaches you not to trust your own conscience and soul. Reject anything that takes away your freedom to ask questions and doubt religious beliefs and doctrine. Reject anything that restricts your ability to love everyone regardless of who they are. Reject those teachings that try to put you in a box with cardboard theological walls that would separate you from your humanity.

If you have experienced such abuse and misdirected teaching and maybe have been rebuked and chided for asking hard questions or have been verbally assaulted by a friend or family member for questioning your beliefs, then read on.

For two decades I taught students in middle school and high school to accept Evangelical dogma. I was a Christian School teacher of the Bible and history. In that role I had a position of respect and authority by which to influence a generation of young people. And influence I did.

I still hear from former students who thank me for the teaching and role model I provided. I am grateful to them for their kind words. Yet, I am still concerned that my role and authority in the classroom may have been misused in the pursuit of an absolute truth and religious dogma that was damaging.

I've talked to many former students that have rejected the Evangelical worldview because it has been damaging to them personally. It didn't give them an abundant life, but a life of guilt, fear, judgment, and condemnation. It is to those students that I think this manuscript will speak.

I offer this book which is a record of my own personal journey of recovery from the evangelical mindset, as a recompense and an offering of restitution to those that are struggling. I dedicate my journey to my former students who may still be questioning, doubting, searching, and evolving in their faith.

I hope you can now understand that doubt IS faith. Doubt is necessary in order to have faith. Faith without doubt is simply blind acceptance of someone else's theology. Doubt can be the motivation and driver that causes faith to grow and deepen. Doubt can assuage the fear that religious authorities use to maintain control of their flocks, burden you with unwarranted guilt, heap condemnation on your heads for being human, keep you in the pews and their coffers full.

To those that have questioned and doubted I say, keep pushing forward and keep on asking questions no matter the cost. It is a journey well-travelled to do so. I can promise you there is life after Evangelicalism. It is life abundant, and Jesus is still there.

I still love every one of you, and I hope this book gives you some hope and encouragement along your own journey.

—"Mr. H."

INTRODUCTION

TO ALL RECOVERING EVANGELICALS

I have found that the source of love, peace and wholeness is not a supernatural human-like religious God up in the sky who comes to me in the form of an interpersonal relationship. Instead, I have found that the most sacred, divine, deeply meaningful and profound experiences I have, come to me as a natural part of my human experience. Jesus himself blurred the lines between what is "divine" and what is "human."[1]

—**Jim Palmer**, Founder of The Center for Non-Religious Spirituality

I AM A RECOVERING Evangelical. The use of the term "Evangelical" is in many ways an unfair label on my part. Not all Evangelicals fit the descriptions and generalizations that I make here. It is not my goal to label all Evangelicals the same and dismiss them out of hand. In fact, my apologies to the Evangelicals who do not identify with the Christian Right, are inclusive and accepting of gay rights, work against the racist tendencies that characterize the heritage of many Evangelical institutions, or those that actively opposed Donald Trump. But it is clear that the Evangelicals as I just described are certainly a minority.

For two decades I taught history in private Christian Schools and can assure you that to be anything except politically conservative is a risk in those institutions. Textbooks published by conservative Christian Colleges were the only acceptable curriculum, and to be anything other than pro-birth and anti-gay marriage was grounds for dismissal. In leaving the Evangelical movement, many former students and parents have asked why I made such an exit. How did I come to these conclusions and why did I make this break?

These are fair questions and deserve a direct answer. But it's not a simple answer and it was a long process. There's a big difference between deciding to leave and knowing where to go. There have been many people and experiences along the way that have shaped my spiritual evolution, which I will share. Leaving the Evangelical faith was also a coming home decision as well.

Evangelicalism was quite different in the 1960s as I was growing up than it is in the 2000s. Perhaps the biggest and most obvious change was the politicization of the Evangelical faith that started in the 1980s although in hindsight I can see that the process started much earlier.

As a young Evangelical in the 1960s and early 70s I never viewed my faith through a political lens. Not a lot of "Jesus People," as we were known, adopted any political stand. If we did, it was more on the liberal side of the spectrum. And by the way, the name "Jesus People" seems so much more inviting today than the term "Christian."

This was an era of anti-war and pro-civil rights movements and Jesus People were just as likely to protest an unjust war or injustice due to segregation and discrimination as attend a prayer meeting. We tended to see Jesus as a revolutionary and counter-cultural icon that allowed us to be anti-establishment with a religious justification.

But with the advent of the religious right in the late 1970s and 80s it was rather stunning for me to learn that you had to vote Republican and support Ronald Reagan to be in the good graces of Evangelical leaders. This trend only accelerated and has worsened in the years since. So, to leave this new version of Evangelicalism by the mid-2000s was like returning to my countercultural roots.

But there is more to it than that. Through rigorous reading and study, I began to reconstruct my view of faith and spirituality that goes beyond my 1960s and 70s roots. Even as a teenager I was captivated by the classics of western civilization, which laid a strong foundation for humanistic thought. At that time I investigated many different religious faiths. I synthesized much from my studies of Judaism and Buddhism in those days at Thomas Jefferson High School and didn't see them as incompatible with the teachings of Jesus. Therefore, even as an adult Evangelical Christian School teacher in the 1980's and 90's, my dogma and approach was tempered by my earlier absorption of broad ideas both religious and secular.

Then in the early 1990s I began a solitary spiritual migration out of Evangelicalism that was aided by many writers. This along with finding communities online of other seekers who were thinking similar thoughts to mine helped me begin the process of "deconstruction" of my Evangelical mind. Here are some of the authors that have had a profound influence on my journey.

M Scott Peck, *The Different Drum* (1978). What stood out from Peck's classic work was his discussion of the "Four Developmental Phases of Spiritual Growth."[2] These four stages resemble the four stages of human development in general. But here is how he described them:

Phase One – Chaotic, Disordered and Reckless: In this phase of spirituality a person is a pretender. They may put on outward clothes of religious life through church attendance or even devotion, but their orientation is totally self-centered, and there is no commitment to any principle beyond the self. It resembles the sociopathic behavior of criminality but emerges in a religious context.

Phase Two – Formal and Institutional: This usually begins with a religious conversion and results in an enthusiastic commitment to religious orthodoxy and dogma. It provides certainty and order out of the chaos and recklessness of phase one, but the individual finds solace in the sense of order and being right. All other views are dismissed based on Biblical or religious texts. Questioning and doubt are not allowed or tolerated within communities of phase two religious people. Many people never allow themselves to outgrow this phase but remain stuck in the comfort of the certainty and order that they have found.

Phase Three – Skepticism and Questioning: The earmark of this phase is a healthy questioning of all that one has learned to that point in life. Adolescents do this into adulthood until they develop their own sense of self. This phase includes the acceptance of doubt, reasoning, skepticism of religious authority including ancient texts, and critical evaluation of one's religious assumptions. This becomes the realm of scientific approaches and even atheistic conclusions for some. For others, this is a transitory phase into a new world of faith and understanding.

Phase Four – Mystical/Communal: This is the realm of moving well beyond the black and white binary understanding of faith, religion and world itself. It is the acceptance and embrace of mystery and lack of having definite, dogmatic pat answers for all questions of life. The difference between "truth" and "fact" becomes apparent to people in this phase and it is home of the connected mind and heart.

Although this conceptualization of spiritual phases may not be perfect it made a great deal of sense to me especially as I moved into the third phase, questioning and skepticism. I found out quickly that this could get you in a lot of trouble in Evangelical circles. But Peck's book motivated me to continue through these developmental stages.

Another author of great importance to me in my spiritual journey is the Catholic monk, **Thomas Merton**. For several years, I read everything I could by Merton including, *Thoughts in Solitude*, which I carried in my pocket continuously, *The Seven Story Mountain*, *No Man Is An Island* and *Contemplative Prayer*.

In many ways Merton was my pathway into Peck's fourth phase of spiritual development, the mystical/communal. In Merton's writing I found hope, solace, contentment and understanding that the dogmatic views of my Evangelical past were not essential for continued spiritual development. I have learned from Merton that a spiritual life is an interior life that breaks open to love those around me. Here is how Merton described it:

> Does God impose a meaning on my life from the outside, through event, custom, routine, law, system, impact with others in society? Or am I called to create from within, with him, with his grace, a meaning which reflects his truth and makes me his "word" spoken freely in my personal situation? My true identity lies hidden in God's call to my freedom and my response to him. This means I must use my freedom in order to love, with full responsibility and authenticity, not merely receiving a form imposed on me by external forces, or forming my own life according to an approved social pattern, but directing my love to the personal reality of my brother, and embracing God's will in its naked, often impenetrable mystery.[3]

Other authors that I have read and benefited recently from their insights and experience include **Frank Schaeffer**, son of the famous evangelist, Francis Schaeffer. Frank's books, *Patience with God: Faith for People Who Don't Like Religion (or Atheism)*, *Crazy for God: How I Grew Up as One of the Elect, Helped Found the Religious Right, and Lived to Take All (or Almost All) of It Back*, and *Why I am an Atheist Who Believes in God: How to give love, create beauty and find peace*, have had a profound impact on my own decision to walk away from Evangelicalism.

In many ways, Frank's writings gave me the courage to begin to speak out about my experiences as well. As an early leader in the Christian Right, Frank and his father, Francis Schaeffer, were key in my own study of Christian theology in the 1970's. But with Frank's rejection of the hard right turn in Evangelical Christianity and his outspokenness about this break in the 1980s, he has given many like me a platform from which to speak as well.

The **Rev. John Shelby Spong**, the late archbishop of the Anglican Church, is one of many leaders of what has come to be called Progressive Christianity. From his writings and others in this movement I've become aware that there really is room for a new distillation of the Christian faith that better fits our 21st Century context. His books that influenced my thinking include, *Biblical Literalism: A Gentile Heresy*; *Reclaiming the Bible for Non-Religious World*; and *The Fourth Gospel, Tales of a Jewish Mystic.*

Recently I have been inspired by the writings of **Jim Palmer**, former evangelical pastor, and now director of "*The Center for Non-Religious Spirituality.*" Jim's experience and clarity around deconstructing one's faith and how to nurture and care for your spiritual growth on the other side is life-giving. I have appreciated his guidance and help.

There are others too numerous to mention but as always, I continue to seek and read and study. As a result of walking away from the Evangelical straight jacket that I found myself in, I have experienced more freedom and contentment spiritually as never before.

The writings presented here were simply a result of journaling from the past 10 or 15 years. Each chapter can stand on its own and you don't have to read the book linearly. You can jump around to chapters that may seem more relevant to you at any given time.

They represent my changing perspective on religion, spirituality, culture and all of life. In pulling them together, they do fall into some natural categories:

> **Part One – Deconstructing Faith Through Doubt**, this section highlights the importance of doubting and questioning beliefs and assumptions you are raised with. The question-

ing led to the deconstruction of my prior beliefs and faith, but the birth of a whole new way of conceptualizing spirituality.

Part Two – Faith and Racial Justice, Becoming Anti-Racist, a new concept of spirituality has allowed me to think about racial injustice in a new way. These essays highlight the changing view of personal bias and racism and my own responsibility for changing the systems that still promote white supremacy.

Part Three – Faith and Gay Rights, Love is Love, Regardless, in the same way I began to look at racial justice differently, I also have had to adjust my views on same sex love and marriage. I thank my daughter for helping me in this transformation. She wrote one chapter about her friend Carla which shows how love wins over hate every time.

Part Four - How Evangelical Ideology Threatens Culture, from my experience in the evangelical movement and Christian Nationalism, there are dangerous and damaging results from this toxic ideology that I highlight in this section. This doesn't mean I condemn all evangelicals, but the ideology that has taken over the movement needs to be exposed.

Part Five – Other Deconstruction "Heresies," this section will cover several other areas of life that are important to me, that have completely changed as a result of my deconstruction and leaving the evangelical church behind. Topics included are humanism, being Prolife, thanking Donald Trump and assorted other ideas.

I invite you to join me on this journey as I share with you my thoughts, struggles, ideas, concerns, and reflections on how and why I am a *Recovering Evangelical*. I sincerely hope you will ask questions about faith, hard questions, and live with the ambiguity of not having all the answers. It is truly transformational and revolutionary.

PART ONE

DECONSTRUCTING FAITH THROUGH DOUBT

ONE

MY PERSONAL JOURNEY

More to the point: the growing universe of the Nones – the new nonreligious – is one of the most spiritually vibrant and provocative spaces in modern life. It is not a world in which spiritual life is absent. It is a world that resists religious excesses and shallows.[1]

—**Krista Tippett,** American journalist, author

IN 1966 I ATTENDED a Billy Graham Crusade meeting in Omaha, Nebraska. I went forward as an 11-year-old boy to give my life to Christ. I became engrossed in the Evangelical movement for the next four decades of my life. In 2005, I walked away from it.

From recent surveys (*Pew Research Center*, 2021), it appears I am not alone. Nearly 3 out of 10 Americans identify themselves as having no religious affiliation.[2] I joined the ranks of the *Nones* which describes people that are not affiliated with any religious organization but who still ascribe to spirituality. It is the fastest growing religious group in America.

The Nones aren't atheists necessarily, but it does mean that many people in the United States are leaving the Evangelical church behind after having spent a lifetime attending services, being involved and devout. Clearly something has happened to make Christianity as a religious institution less appealing or satisfying to people in the 21st Century.

It is even more profound for the millennial generation. Fewer and fewer are attending or maintaining an association with organized religion. There are literally thousands and tens of thousands of people who are experiencing what I have experienced which is a growing sense of irrelevance and dissatisfaction with what has been called Evangelical Christianity.

I am a recovering Evangelical. What does that mean? It means I'm recovering from decades of not trusting my own instincts, accepting biblical literalism, abandoning the *us vs. them* mentality, and rejecting scientific evidence. In a word, I'm unlearning the indoctrination of a narrow and authoritarian mindset. It also involves forgetting and leaving fear and guilt behind as a life motivation. I'm still trying to figure it out but perhaps a short biography here would be a good place to start.

My bona fides as an Evangelical go back to my childhood and youth in Iowa as I suspect most people in Middle America can attest. I grew up in a conservative Christian church and as I mentioned, went forward at a Billy Graham crusade and gave my life to Christ.

From there I became totally immersed in the Evangelical world through youth groups at church, Christian coffee houses, home churches, the charismatic movement, and later, Bible College, and seminary. I had a real passion for anything Christian and anything related to the Bible which of course meant accepting it as absolute, inerrant, and inspired by God.

I did my share of witnessing to people which usually amounted to giving out a tract or sharing my story and then telling people what they needed to do to go to heaven and avoid hell. I was a real Jesus freak of the 1960s and early 70s.

Although I flirted with the idea of becoming a pastor something inside told me I was better suited to becoming a teacher. I'm glad I listened to that voice. I went to a Lutheran College and earned a BA in teaching, history, and social studies, became a Christian School teacher in 1979 and taught in private

Evangelical Christian schools for the next 20 years. I taught young people about history, social studies and indoctrinated them with the Christian Worldview. Later, I earned a master's degree in School Administration and spent several years as a Christian School principal and leader in the Christian School movement.

It was early in my career in the Christian School that I found "God's will for my life" in terms of a wife. She was also a teacher, and we seemed like a providential match. The people around us echoed this sentiment that our relationship was ordained by God. We were married, had two beautiful children, and pretended to be a happily married Christian couple. I continued to work in Christian Schools, went to church religiously, and taught Sunday school and served on various committees.

Seems perfect, right?

This scenario is repeated innumerably in Christian subculture, along with the narrative of happily-ever-after. But there were two problems with this grand illusion. First, for all those years that I was walking around as an Evangelical using the Bible to justify condemning those that were non-Christian and indoctrinating kids with a Biblical worldview, I had major doubts and questions myself that simply could not be answered.

The certainty and unbending absolutism of the Evangelical faith fell short in the light of modern experience and science. A lot of issues simply did not square with the Evangelical narrative I had spent my life teaching. I chose to ignore most of this and do intellectual contortions to make it work.

But these intellectual exercises could not alleviate the vexing doubt I felt that everything I had taught about Christianity in the Evangelical tradition was true. From the inerrancy of the Bible to condemnations on those who were from other faith traditions, and believing in a literal creation, it was becoming increasingly difficult to defend and justify an approach to life that claimed absolute certainty for all people and all issues for all time. I had swallowed Evangelical Christianity hook-lines and sinkers but was having a great deal of spiritual indigestion.

I did what most Evangelicals do, stuff it, ignore it and get busy saving souls.

Doubt is a cardinal sin in the Evangelical world. You would do better to become an alcoholic or drug addict, which would result in a grand testimonial about God's redemption and forgiveness, than admit to real doubt about the inspiration of the scripture. The former was cause for an enthusiastic round of *Amens* while the latter was cause for wagging a finger and shaking of the head in divine condemnation.

The second thing that shattered my grand illusion was the dissolution of my marriage. Being a leader in a Christian ministry and getting a divorce was practically an unpardonable sin.

I understood divorce quite well and was never inclined to look down on those who experienced it. I had grown up in a single-parent home with two brothers and my mother. My parents were divorced when I was five years-old and I knew the pain and disruption that a breakup like that can cause.

My mother was a dedicated Christian and the reason for me or my brothers becoming anything of value at all. I knew her faith had sustained her. But in the Christian Ministry divorce was an existential crisis.

I even had a not-so-well-meaning parent of one of my students enter my office one day to announce that God had told him that I should resign due to my impending divorce. *Thanks for the empathy and support fella*! It was odd how God was "speaking" something different to him than to me. Both of us couldn't be right or perhaps God couldn't make up his mind.

The issue for me at that time was much more a personal crisis of faith. The God's-will-for-my-life-spouse and marriage had just run head-on into the reality that we really weren't well suited for each other and had grown far apart.

How could it be that God's will was so different than what I was experiencing in real life? And frankly, so painful? I thought God wanted us to be happy and to be an example of Christ and the church. And having grown up in a single-parent home I didn't want my own kids to experience the heartache and trauma that comes with a family breakup.

In addition to all the cognitive dissonance that the divorce brought upon me, the questions and doubts about my Evangelical faith came crashing down at the same time. The certainty was gone. It was a watershed moment. My faith was undergoing a radical shift. I could not return to the certainty and arrogance of my Evangelical past no matter how hard I tried. The Evangelical edifice I had spent my life building was collapsing on my head. I was forced finally, to face the nagging questions and doubts that had been tucked away in my mind for so many years.

I decided to confront my doubts, head-on. Starting in the early 1990s I began questioning everything. I started investigating the doubts I had ignored and buried for so long. I did hold on to the vestiges of Evangelical faith for the next several years, like holding onto a dream that was fading away.

Leaving Christian school ministry, a year after my divorce, I entered public education as a teacher and administrator. It turned out to be the best move of my life for many reasons both professionally and personally. For the next ten years I felt myself evolving rapidly away from my Evangelical roots. Getting out of the Evangelical greenhouse or hothouse was an important step. Each day that passed my previously held Evangelical beliefs felt increasingly absurd and I could no longer buy into many of the assumptions of that approach to faith.

I attended other conservative churches until it finally dawned on me in 2005 that I was no longer an Evangelical. I had outgrown it. I was in a conservative church, but I just couldn't reconcile myself any longer to that expression of faith.

The final trigger came when the pastor was on a sabbatical and the elders were asking various laypeople to take a turn in the pulpit to share "what God had laid on our heart." When they asked me, I literally panicked and realized that I couldn't do it because it would be a lie.

I knew what they were expecting, and if I had shared what was really on my heart and mind that week, they would have been shocked at what they heard. So, I left the church not out of anger or acrimony, but because I just didn't want to live a lie anymore. I didn't want to pretend. I was feeling so out of place in a conservative church that I just could no longer do it.

Many of you will understand what I'm talking about when I say I was no longer comfortable. The code language used in Evangelical churches can create guilt and defensiveness in those not used to it or who have come to doubt the veracity of the phrases.

It wasn't the "God bless you" or "peace be with you" that I am talking about. It is the presumptiveness of comments like, "God is speaking to me about...." Or "I think God's will for your life is..." It was hard to not question what God's voice sounded like or respond with some other sarcastic comment.

So, there you have it. I left Evangelical Christianity after several decades and time invested in a way of life and thinking. However, that process, as I reflect on it now, began even years before that and continues today.

It would be a mistake to suggest that I have rejected faith. I have not made the jump to atheism as some have. But I have attempted to redefine faith and to find new meaning to spirituality that goes beyond the Evangelical framework.

Do I consider myself a Christian? I do, but I suspect most Evangelicals would call me a backslider and heretic. That is fine as I suspect I am in good company. But my goal isn't to condemn those who are still of the Evangelical worldview. I have many friends, former students, and family members who I respect a great deal that are still of the Evangelical persuasion.

But here is what I have discovered; doubts and uncertainties about religious belief are normal and should be welcomed. If everyone were honest, they would admit to having these questions and doubts.

They can be a doorway into a new configuration of an ancient religious faith that has begun to decline in relevancy. I believe by questioning, seeking and exploring, people will grow in their faith, perhaps a post-Evangelical faith. I discovered that doubt was the doorway to this new pathway.

What follows in these pages are the writings that reflect my deconstruction process of the Evangelical faith and the emergence of a new understanding. This isn't a grand revelation, and it certainly isn't meant as a blueprint for anyone else. But I do suspect that many people are expressing doubts and have questions about things they have taken for granted as true but no longer make sense or provide fulfillment. I hope if you are one of these "doubters" you will find solace and a place to rest along your own journey.

These pages are here to let you know you aren't alone and that it is okay to question your faith, seek new answers, deconstruct what you've been taught and find new ways to express your faith. So many others are on this road, and you are not alone. I offer my thoughts here on a variety of topics that reflect my changing perspective and new freedom to explore these ideas. It is a personal inner journey, but my desire is that it gives you hope.

Deconstruction can be a painful process. Those around you may not understand and even condemn you for it. You may feel afraid to share your new perspectives and understandings as I had for a long time. But knowing that others have traveled the same road, I hope it will give you strength and courage to pursue your own recovery. That's what it is, a recovery. It is a recovery of your own humanity.

Two

AM I CONNECTED

A 21ST CENTURY VIEW OF ANCIENT TRUTH

Only when we see ourselves in our true human context, as members of a race which is intended to be one organism and "one body," will we begin to understand the positive importance not only of the successes but of the failures and accidents in our lives . . . Therefore the meaning of my life is not to be looked for merely in the sum total of my achievements. It is seen only in the complete integration of my achievements and failures with the achievements and failures of my own generation, and society, and time.[1]

—**Thomas Merton**, *No Man is an Island*

THE MOST IMPORTANT PHRASE heard these days anywhere in the world is this: "Am I connected?" The Holy Grail of existence now is for everyone to be connected to a network all the time. It can be annoying, troubling, and even ridiculous in comparison to the more important issues of living, but it is understandable. It is understandable not from a technical point of view but from a spiritual point of view.

Why are people so desirous of being connected to their devices? Is it the device that holds some magic sway? I don't think so. It is likely the connection to the people, friends, groups, and information that the device affords so easily and continually by being connected to the internet. It is so important to humans that they risk car accidents and walking into signposts on the sidewalk to achieve this prized reality of connection.

But the devotion to which people commit themselves to seek this connection begs the question of "why?" Why is this so important? Are we that isolated? Do we need something more than what reality can provide? Why do humans crave connection?

This is a fitting analogy for a description of faith that I have come to accept. Most people define faith as a set of beliefs. Ask someone what their faith means, and they will launch into a recitation of their church's statement of faith, the Apostles Creed, or some other propositional list of beliefs.

What has become clear to me is that one's propositional beliefs do not make the sum-total of what one would call faith. Faith goes beyond mere ascent to a set of propositions or doctrines. In fact, I have come to believe that doctrines can get in the way of discovering faith.

I have known too many Christians in my lifetime that were strict adherents to a set of doctrines but were to be blunt, simply awful people. Anyone with a history of church life will understand what I just said. No need to elaborate. Believing in the creeds and even memorizing and reciting them does no good to anyone if they are hateful, deceitful, or cruel people.

Separating faith from a set of beliefs has been a truly transformational process for me. There are several consequences to doing this that I want to share.

The process of separating faith from belief has allowed me to essentially not care what another person's beliefs are. I no longer need to divide people into different camps based on their doctrinal statement, beliefs or non-beliefs, or the religion they adhere to. I no longer bear the responsibility of setting them straight when it comes to theological discussions.

This is not just a non-denominational approach, and it goes well beyond just trying to get along. If I no longer define faith as a set of beliefs, I no longer need to divide folks into *me vs. them* or our group vs. that other group. There is no "other," but faith promotes the "we" of all humanity because all humans have and experience faith.

Religions are culturally defined institutions that people use to attempt to seek, define and explain the divine. My religious tradition, Christianity, is culturally derived. If I had been born in India, I would likely be a Hindu or Buddhist, or if I had been born in Iran, I would likely be a Muslim. To understand faith is to understand that a culturally derived set of beliefs does not give anyone a corner on the market to truth nor the right to condemn those who weren't born and acculturated in a particular belief system.

Faith, when understood as a connection, helps me to understand that all people regardless of their beliefs, culture, or even non-beliefs, are responding to the same impulse that all humans share, which is the desire for connectedness.

I think it is culturally arrogant to suggest there is only one religious tradition by which all people of all time and places must subscribe or they will be condemned to the eternal fires of hell. This idea has played out in history more as a political argument to justify imperialist policies and invading other countries, ostensibly for their own good. It only serves to separate people, not to connect them.

So long as people define faith as a set of beliefs there will be division, friction and fighting over whose beliefs are right. And in the arena of religion which inevitably seeps into politics, this is an unwinnable battle. We will be destined to continuous and constant fighting and war until we are able to give up the insane idea that somehow, one culturally derived set of beliefs is superior or better than another.

If faith is not the same thing as propositional belief, then what is faith? How is it defined and understood? I've already stated that faith is connectedness. But that can be vague.

This is a hard one to answer because I don't believe it can be defined. Even the Bible defines faith as something unknowable. *"Now faith is the assurance of things hoped for, the conviction of things not seen."* (Hebrews 11) Something that is not seen can hardly be defined. Something I hope for has no physical reality, it exists in my head or my heart.

But the one thing we can say about this verse is it doesn't define faith by a doctrinal belief, creed, or theology. In other words, the Bible does not define faith as the Apostles Creed or the Evangelical list of non-negotiables that all true believers must believe. I hope people of religious belief can move forward and beyond such a shallow definition of faith. The Bible doesn't support it and it makes no sense.

I can describe what faith is like when it is experienced. Something that cannot be rationally defined can still be experienced, so it isn't accurate to say that faith is a fiction or myth. It is like one of those things in life that you know when it happens but can't quite put your finger on it to define it.

The best example I can think of in my own life and career is the perennial attempt at defining what a good teacher is. During my 30 years as an educator, legislative policy makers have constantly tried to determine how to evaluate teachers and identify which ones are good, better, and best. All the schemes to do this have so far failed miserably to provide an absolute model or scale of what a good teacher is.

But for students and teachers alike it is one of those things you know when you see it because you've experienced the effects of what a good teacher does. And sometimes the effects are not realized until much later. That is the same dilemma when it comes to faith, it is undefinable, but you know it when you see it and experience the effect of it.

If faith is more of an experience than a mental understanding this opens the door to the criticism of reducing faith to mere sentimentality or ecstatic emotionalism. This is not what I am referring to and it illustrates the problem of trying to even describe faith. Using words and language is inherently rational so any attempt to use words and language by me will certainly fall short.

But I'll still try because the attempt is worth it no matter how inadequate it might be.

When I say faith is an experience what I mean is that we experience faith by connections. Connections are the events, experiences, and moments in life when conscious human beings become aware of our interrelationships to the world around us in ways we have not understood. These connections give me a sense of wonder, fulfillment, contentment, and joy. It is the ultimate sense of being human. Jesus said he came to give life, and life abundantly. The most abundant life I have ever experienced is when I have felt deep abiding connections.

Some of the connections that I have experienced that expand the sense of my own humanness are those such as when I have held my newborn children for the first time.

Or the connection of friendship in a way that has caused me to both laugh with joy in their presence and grieve with sorrow when there is loss.

I have felt connected to the whole of the universe through moments of transcendent reflection upon nature, the stars and my own place within the cosmos.

It is at those moments that the connections I feel give me the sense of wholeness, oneness, integration, and completeness so that I can say without reservation, I lack nothing, and I desire nothing more.

Faith is expressed in the connections that cause us to reach further than we ever thought possible, to become more human than we have ever dreamed and to view the world as a single entity, like seeing it from space where there are no boundaries, religions, or cultures. There are just humans sharing a planet within a connected universe.

Faith causes me to cherish the physical world around me because I am connected to it. I am literally grounded in faith when I engage in environmental care.

As I write this, I am sitting on a condominium deck on the coast of Florida watching and listening to the waves from the Gulf of Mexico crash and move upon the shoreline just about 100 yards from me. How many people have said they feel a connection to the sea? To a lake? To the mountains? Or to the beauty even of an Iowa corn field? These connections help us to know we are not alone or isolated. We are part of a oneness that encompasses not only all of humanity but the whole universe.

I believe this is at the core of our desire to return to space travel, not just for scientific information alone which is cause enough to go, but in a spiritual sense I think we feel oneness with the universe from where our whole existence began. Connections drive us to do many things that are wonderful, fulfilling, and enduring. Acting on faith, our sense of connections brings achievement, healing, compassion, and progress.

Compassion is key! Connectedness enhances our sense of seeking to help, serve, protect, and love others. It is why a stranger can risk his own life to help save the life of another. Faith in this sense does away with any distinctions between human beings such as race, gender, creed, or beliefs. Perhaps this is the ultimate meaning of the death of Christ, by giving himself up to death on behalf of others it created the greatest example of how we can reintegrate our own souls. The Bible says, "Christ in you, the hope of glory." It is unseen and cannot be reduced to a simple list of beliefs which pales in comparison to the inner connection of my being with all that is.

Faith is an experience that is expansive, not exclusive.

Faith creates wholeness, not fragmentation.

Faith promotes healing from brokenness.

Faith doesn't divide me from people but connects me to them.

And ultimately, it is faith that connects me to God, and I begin to learn that God is not a separate thing or entity.

As Jesus said, "I and the Father are one," so I can also begin to integrate my being with God. This won't happen through a theology, statement of doctrine or quoting Bible verses. It only happens through a connection with the divine which already exists in me as part of my humanity. I am not separated from God but am one with God through faith.

THREE

FAITH

I DON'T THINK THAT WORD MEANS WHAT YOU THINK IT MEANS

For He can well be loved, but he cannot be thought. By love he can be grasped and held, but by thought, neither grasped nor held. And therefore, though it may be good at times to think specifically of the kindness and excellence of God, and though this may be a light and a part of contemplation, all the same, in the work of contemplation itself, it must be cast down and covered with a cloud of forgetting. And you must step above it stoutly but deftly, with a devout and delightful stirring of love, and struggle to pierce that darkness above you; and beat on that thick cloud of unknowing with a sharp dart of longing love, and do not give up, whatever happens.

—The Cloud of Unknowing

MY FAVORITE LINE FROM the classic movie *The Princess Bride* is this, "I don't think that word means what you think it means." I don't think that the word *faith* today means what most people think it does. I'll extend the concept of faith as a connection from the last chapter and take it a step farther and connect faith to the concept of doubt. To have faith is to doubt! It feels counter-intuitive and contradictory, but once you understand the connection between doubt and faith, it is transformational.

My Evangelical friends all define the word faith as a right belief. Right belief in the deity of Jesus Christ, his virgin birth, the resurrection of Jesus from the dead and the need to ask Jesus into your heart to have a personal relationship with him. But the right relationship is based on the right thought or belief.

I call this the Christian Cult of Certainty. It is rooted in the belief that if I get a set of propositional truths right, then I am right with God. This certainty serves as a security blanket or crutch in the face of an unpredictable and ambiguous world. But it also serves as a weapon to justify imposing Christian beliefs on society, communities, and other nations.

The cornerstone proposition that must be believed to have true faith in the Evangelical world is in the inerrancy and inspiration of the Bible and one cannot possibly have faith unless you accept, with certainty and absolute assurance, that the Bible is the Word of God.

I don't think that word means what they think it means. In fact, I have learned that faith is the opposite of certainty and absolute belief.

If all a person needs to do is accept the Bible as 100% true and the propositional doctrines of the Church as the embodiment of that truth, then it isn't about faith at all. It is simply about the acceptance of something outside of myself. Faith is something that someone cooked up many centuries ago and all that is required is my cognitive acceptance.

Faith as propositional truth simply requires an intellectual ascent or endorsement that can never be doubted or questioned. Someone else did the hard work of defining faith and you only need to accept it unquestioningly. Faith isn't about searching or struggling with mystery, it is simply a cognitive exercise.

Faith as intellectual assent makes for an unstable or insecure faith. Faith in this sense reminds me of a big game of *Jenga*. Christians have created this huge stack of wooden blocks called faith statements. And if you start to pull them out one by one you risk having the whole structure come crashing down. Therefore, Christians feel compelled to fight for every block in the structure lest the structure become less and less stable.

Sometimes science pulls a block out from the structure, say, with evidence of evolution, and Christians find that they are arguing for an antiquated view of the universe that defies all known scientific evidence. Christians defend these faith statements as absolute truths that are to be defended and believed but never questioned. They cannot risk under any circumstances any uncertainty.

The question to ponder is in what way is certainty the same as faith?

I propose that faith has nothing to do with believing anything as objective truth. For me and for many Christians in history, faith is *unknowing*. It is the opposite of knowing something for sure and having absolute certainty about a religious idea. Faith in this sense is rooted in doubt.

Faith is coming face to face with mystery and responding with "I don't know." It accepts uncertainty and embraces ambiguity.

Evangelicals believe that to compromise the cult of certainty they compromise the whole faith. That is the result of defining faith as the right belief.

Even in the face of contradictory evidence you must stubbornly argue for the right beliefs. It results in the marginalization and increasing irrelevance of Christianity as its adherents become more and more strident and militant in their beliefs and I might add, appear silly in doing so. This likely explains the rapid growth of the Nones in the 21st century. Evangelical beliefs are becoming harder and harder to explain and defend as more scientific knowledge emerges.

Christians complain about the stereotypical depictions of them in the popular media, but one needs to ask who is at fault? Perhaps it is self-inflicted.

If faith isn't a set of propositional truths to believe, then just what is it? Redefining the word faith has turned the whole equation upside down. I have already explained faith as connections in chapter 2. But we can now extend that connection to embracing the unknowable.

For me faith is a way of reaching out to the unknowable and that which can never be defined. It is never certain, always doubts and never definitively answers the questions of mystery. Faith cannot create creeds, canons, or other certainties within religion because these cannot be proven or verified.

Faith allows humans to contemplate that which is unknowable and cannot be explained through scientific proof or observation.

Faith is a disposition that causes me to search and consider and even hope in those things I cannot see. Faith like this creates not only hope but just as important, humility. This humility requires that I treat others with grace because they are confronted with the same "unknowing" as I. We are all in the same boat of uncertainty.

The purpose of faith then isn't to define anything. The purpose of faith is to search, question, and continue to search. It is an internal disposition toward that which is unknowable. It is not an external acceptance of a creed or biblical text.

Religions try defining God and use their definition to attain certainty. Faith questions God and lives with ambiguity. And living with ambiguity is perhaps the uncomfortableness of faith. It doesn't bring closure or final resolution and the one thing Evangelicals seek most is closure or finality.

Faith is what allows me to continue to seek connection with all that is unknowable including God.

Faith gives strength to people in dire and severe situations and allows them to continue to live, love and forgive.

Faith is more a state of being as opposed to a state of knowing.

Faith as a state of being is expansive, inclusive, and life-giving because it doubts and seeks connection, not definition.

Faith as a state of being seeks to build up, not to separate people into opposing groups and condemn those that don't accept Jesus into their hearts in some formulistic way.

Faith as a state of being defies the Cult of Certainty that characterizes Christianity so much today which presents Christianity as arrogant to non-adherents.

Faith in unknowing is a humble approach to life and spirituality that allows each person to seek the unknowable in a way that builds inner strength.

Finally, faith is simply part of being human and to embrace faith is to embrace our humanity which is after all, what Jesus did.

Back to *the Princess Bride*. "I don't think that word means what you think it means." So long as Christians try to define faith as a set of propositional statements Christianity will be a force for division and tribalism.

Rather than the universal vision of all humans that Jesus talked about, Christianity will continue to be used as a sledgehammer to beat people into the mode of right belief. The Bible will continue to be used as a cudgel to force conformity and obedience and even discrimination. Faith defined in this way kills life.

This is likely the reason so many people feel exhausted, beat down and even abused in their church experience. There is constant pressure and tension to accept correct beliefs to be accepted and told that you are now in God's good standing. This is emotional hard work, because it creates such dissonance with people. It can be tiresome and for many it can lead to depression.

For me, once I began to redefine faith as a state of being, the freedom to question and search became quite inspiring. I haven't drifted into atheism at all although I can understand why some people do.

Atheism simply ignores the inherent faith as a state of being that is inside each of us. You can easily ignore faith and only accept a way of thinking based on science and that does make some intellectual sense. Some days that is very appealing. It explains the title of one of Frank Schaeffer's books: "Why I Am an Atheist Who Believes in God." It makes complete sense.

But I have been inspired to seek further and question harder than ever before and consequently I feel that my faith has grown not because I have defined anything, but because I have questioned everything, and grown more comfortable with the uncertainty and ambiguity.

I'm finding that to not be certain, and to not have the answers is okay. I still consider myself a Christian even though most of the creeds I have come to question, and I don't believe in the inerrancy of the Bible any longer. It's okay, I can live with the uncertainty.

Faith has a whole lot more to do with the type of human being I want to become, and how I am treating those I love, and those I meet for the first time, and the stranger that is different from me.

Faith has helped me to see that being human to the highest degree possible is following the example that Jesus set.

That is GOOD NEWS!

FOUR

FAITH AS BELIEF OR FAITH AS BEING?

If you stay in your faith you're going to get paid. I am now living in my reward.

—**Joyce Meyer,** Prosperity Gospel Preacher

There is a miracle in your mouth. If you want to change your world, start by changing your words. If you'll learn how to speak the right words, and keep the right attitude, God will turn that situation around.

—**Joel Osteen,** Prosperity Gospel Preacher

THERE IS FAITH. AND then there is what people say that faith is. The two are dramatically different.

I want to tell you about a friend of mine from High School. I'm going to use the name David, since I still want to respect the privacy of his wife and children, and probably grandchildren by now. You see, David died a few years after we graduated from the same high school. I was David's best man at his wedding and David and his wife had two children within a couple of years.

But what I want to share with you is something that David said to me from his hospital bed as he lay dying from cancer. Some people had been coming to visit David and prayed for him and "claimed" his healing. It was their view of faith that you can "name it and claim it." In other words, faith is about having the right mental attitude toward God, and believing hard enough so that God will grant your wishes. It is the heart of the so-called "prosperity gospel." More about that in a moment.

Let me tell you a bit more about David.

David and I became friends through our local church youth group. I was surprised when David came to church because having been an acquaintance of his prior to that at school, he seemed to be in the "tough crowd." He was a hoodlum biker type, which in that era was something you wanted to steer clear of, if you knew better.

I think one of David's other friends invited him to church, witnessed to him, and he ended up giving his life to Christ in a conversion experience. It was in the church youth group and associated social activities that he and I became friends and began to hang out together.

Most of our other friends went to the High School across town. It was the "upper class" high school where kids with big houses and rich families went to school. I doubt that was universally true, but it was the impression of the time. David and I and a couple of others from the youth group were relegated to the "working class" high school on the west end of town, near the river. Sometimes we were called "river rats." But David and I palled around at school and of course attended youth group meetings and activities.

David was not a studious fellow and he and I were an unlikely friendship. I was interested in school and earned a pretty good grade average. David cared very little about school, and I noticed he had a hard time reading books sometimes. In fact, one time he asked me to go plead with a teacher to not fail him in a literature class we were both assigned to. I did go in and plead his case and tried to get the teacher to at least give him a break and a barely passing "D" grade. She appreciated my attempt, but said that she just couldn't do it because, well, David hadn't even handed in one assignment. Later when I became a teacher, I understood her predicament. It would have been wrong, unethical, and unfair to David to inflate his grade.

I don't remember if David ever graduated from High School but I think he must have sooner or later. But one thing he was good at was cars and motorcycles. He could change brakes, tune a car engine, and seemed to have no problem reading a car technical manual. David was a street-smart sort of guy.

The thing I remember most about David is he had a heart of gold. He loved the underdog and was always available to help someone that needed help. He found ways to talk to people in his natural, unassuming verbiage about Jesus. He wasn't pushy, but he did seem to break through to a few people that were his biker associations. He never turned his back on them either after becoming a Christian. David was a loyal friend. I think his changed life made an impression on them more than anything and I never heard any of them tease him for having "religion" at least not in a mean sort of way.

After I graduated from high school I went to a Bible college to learn as much as I could about the Bible. It was only about a year out of High School that I heard from David that he was getting married. He had met a young lady from our youth group and they had been going together for a long time, so I wasn't surprised. I was surprised that he asked me to be his best man and frankly I was honored to do so. So sometime in the mid-1970's I attended David's wedding and saw he and his bride off to their new life together.

It was about that time that we all became involved in a Christian Fellowship home church that grew out of the "charismatic movement." The "faith" movement it was sometimes called or the "word of faith" movement. Many of my prior youth group friends who were now adults, were getting on in this movement and I joined up too. I had my doubts and reservations about the whole thing, but I did my best to pretend to be "one of them." Going away to college put some distance between me and some of the worst aspects of this group and the larger movement and for that I was glad.

David and his wife were involved in this fellowship group and pretty soon they had a baby. If I recall, I think they ended up with two children. By 1980 I had gotten married and started my career as a teacher in a nearby city. And by 1983, along came my first child. So as lives get busy you lose or at least slow down your contact with old friends. But they are still your friends.

That is why it was a shock when I later found out that David had cancer and didn't have long to live. My heart broke for him and his wife and children. He was a great father and husband. As the cancer progressed David was in the hospital, and I knew I needed to go see him as he didn't have much longer to live.

As I entered his room it was just him and me, and I could see immediately he was failing. I told David I was so sorry this was happening to him. He looked at me and said, "I guess I just don't have enough faith." I asked what he meant, and he said others that had come by to pray with him told him they had "claimed" his healing, but it was up to him to have enough faith so that God could heal him. Since he wasn't getting any better he assumed it was his own fault and he didn't have enough faith.

I was shocked when I heard him say that. Then I was angry, and then...livid. I kept my composure for his sake, but I told David in no uncertain terms those people were just wrong, this wasn't his fault and he should not feel guilty about it. I told him I had no idea why this was happening to him but I knew for sure it wasn't due to a lack of faith on his part. I felt horrible for David. And then I wondered what kind of people would heap that sort of guilt on a dying man?

And that is where I want to go with this story. The definition of faith that so many in the evangelical movement have adopted is equated with right belief. Having right beliefs and believing hard enough that God will intercede on your behalf is how faith is defined, particularly in the current charismatic and apostolic movements that are associated with Christian Nationalism.

I don't think this is faith so much as it is wishful thinking. And it is very narcissistic. To believe that any given human has the ability to affect the actions of a "sovereign God" if they believed hard enough is incredibly arrogant.

And what kind of God sets around waiting to see if humans will believe hard enough to satisfy his need for attention so that he will then decide to deliver them from their suffering? And if they don't believe enough or in the right way then just too bad. Truth is, this isn't "God" and it isn't "faith."

This attitude turns faith into a commodity that you can acquire if you pray hard enough, give enough money, volunteer enough of your time, and sacrifice enough of your life to "serve God." The more you do these outward things, supposedly the more faith you have.

Faith is something to be chased, earned and even something to be bargained for. Have enough faith and God will spare your life David. If you aren't healed, then you just didn't pray through hard enough or believe enough or maybe didn't give enough money to God. Your death is your own fault. This view of faith is cruel, heartless and is manipulated and exploited by people many times for their own financial gain.

In the 1970's it was the Godfather of the faith movement Oral Roberts who popularized this message and made a cool $110 million in annual revenue doing so. The message was clear, send me money, believe hard enough, and God will bless you many times over.

Today it is people like Creflo Dollar, T.D. Jakes, Joel Olsteen and Paula White that are filling their pockets with multiple millions of dollars by preaching this "good news for me and bankruptcy for thee" gospel. They prey on the desperate, the ignorant, the elderly, the people at the bottom of the social scale to turn over their hard-earned money and empty their bank accounts so that they can have private jets and mansions. Those are the signs of God's favor after all because they have enough faith, and you can have it too if you would just have enough faith and believe hard enough.

By extension, this message also makes poverty, illness, and bad fortune the sign of a lack of faith and God's disfavor. It victimizes the victims in life, and that brings me back to my friend David.

It was perhaps when I saw the direct impact this distorted message had on my friend, that I began to slowly back away from the whole movement, and eventually evangelical Christianity itself. There were other reasons too but looking at my friend lying in a hospital bed dying and blaming himself for a lack of faith convinced me then that having that view and definition of faith was hokum and at worst, it was evil.

I have had to deconstruct my whole view of faith over the past 30 or 40 years. It took a long time. And when I think of David's life and the goodness he represented, and the impact he had on the people around him by just being true to himself, I realized he was being faith all the time. David didn't need more faith. He was *being* faith by his life and example. And that is the difference. Faith isn't what you believe, it is what you are . . . it is being, not believing. And with that we all have enough faith, there is never a deficit or shortage.

FIVE

LESSONS LEARND FROM VBS

"GOD IS LIKE WHAT?"

Fix reason firmly in her seat, and call to her tribunal every fact, every opinion. Question with boldness even the existence of a God; because, if there be one, he must more approve of the homage of reason, than that of blindfolded fear.

—**Thomas Jefferson** (letter to his nephew, Peter Carr)

EACH SUMMER AS I drive by church after church and see banners advertising a week-long Vacation Bible School. These banners always bring back vivid memories for me of my childhood when my two brothers and I would be shipped off to Vacation Bible School (VBS as it was known) by our poor single-parent mother. I know she had our best interest in mind, but I can't help thinking now, after being a parent of two children myself, that it might have been more for her best interest than it was ours.

She meant well but reflecting on those experiences of day after day, being told Bible story after Bible story, the impact could be shocking and even horrific for a kid at the impressionable age of 7 to 12 years old. I mean we learned some crazy stuff about what people did, what God commanded, and how weird life was in the Bible.

Oh, there were the fun things we got to do like build a Biblical temple out of popsicle sticks or make dioramas of the Battle of Jericho although, I never quite understood what the people of Jericho did wrong to have the Israelites and God destroy their city so indiscriminately. But you never asked such questions. If you did there was "the look" as if you had committed an unpardonable sin. The reality was I don't think the teacher-volunteers knew how to respond.

What follows are the lessons that I learned about God and how the universe worked at VBS. Most of this is based on a literal view of the Bible which was an article of faith at the church I attended and which I have come to learn makes many of these stories absurd.

It takes a contortionist to defend them by any modern standard. But that is what our teachers at VBS did although usually, they simply read the lesson from the Vacation Bible School manual shipped out from denomination-central for that year. To make the lessons more interesting they had flannel graph characters. Raise your hand if you know what a flannel graph is.

So, here goes:

Lesson 1 – God told Abraham to sacrifice his son, Isaac. In other words, Human Sacrifice is okay.—Genesis 22

This story terrified me and almost made me glad I didn't have a father. What if God got it in his head to tell my father to build an altar and sacrifice me; although not being the oldest I thought I might be okay. For some reason in the Bible first-born sons were always the one they targeted. Plus, I figured I could outrun any adult. Truly these thoughts raced through my mind as I heard this lesson. No kidding.

When one looks at the psychology of this story it raises several questions about the nature of God and the impression of God we all embraced. Of course, I had heard the story before, and I knew God was playing a trick on Abraham and at the last moment God would stop Abraham from killing his son.

Abraham was totally willing to muder his son. It didn't help me develop a lot of confidence in God. Why would God trick Abraham like that? Was God really that insecure that he would force Abraham to choose between his son and God? Why would Abraham think that human sacrifice was even okay? Why would anyone obey a God that demanded a human sacrifice? Isn't that what the God of Israel was against? "Thou shalt not kill." This was a very confusing story to a child and as an adult I'm still a bit confused by it. I can't say that it encouraged me to follow God but more to run and hide.

Lesson 2 – God tells the Israelites to kill all Amalekites, every man, woman, child and animal. In other words, Genocide is good, if you are on God's team.—I Samuel 15

Apparently, genocide was alright with God but you'd better be on the right team. I knew the Amalekites were bad people. I mean I learned how they mistreated the Israelites after they came out of Egypt and they were on the Hebrew's land that God was giving to them. They were usually in cahoots with those awful Canaanites. I learned that God favored certain people over others, many times for incidental reasons like, "hey, you guys are in the wrong place."

I also learned that God was thorough and didn't want to leave any one of them alive including the animals. But then I worried about the animals because, well, they hadn't bothered anyone. They were innocent. Why would God want the animals killed too? Why did God want all these people killed including the children? I mean, they could be out there playing in the neighborhood and suddenly, the Israelites would come out of nowhere and kill them all. How was that fair?

I didn't know the word genocide at that age but in comparing this event to all the genocidal events of even recent history, this one stands right up there. Again, this story terrified me and didn't endear me to God at all. But we did build some cool stuff with popsicle sticks.

Lesson 3 – God is jealous. (Deuteronomy 6:15) Wait, why does God need to be jealous?

> *. . . for the Lord your God, who is among you, is a jealous God and his anger will burn against you, and he will destroy you from the face of the land.*

I heard this verse and several others like it countless times during Vacation Bible School and Sunday school too. I wasn't sure then what to think about it, and probably just took it in stride, as in, "ok, God gets really angry if we put someone or something else before him." Got it.

But here is one story I could never figure out. I had a good friend in my hometown whose brother was several years older than us. He was a fantastic baseball player. When he graduated from high school, he was offered a contract to the New York Yankees farm team, the *New York Yankees* for crying out loud!

In those days they had Mickey Mantle, Roger Maris, and all the other heroes. But he turned it down to go to Bible College to become a pastor. I had nothing against that idea, but he gave up what he loved to do, what he was gifted to do by God I assume, to do something he seemed not very happy to do. But the justification was because, "God is a jealous God." Jealous of what? The New York Yankees?

This one I could never, and still can't figure out. Why would God give someone the gift that this fellow had only to deny him the chance to use it for God's glory even, to do something else? And then to say that the reason is that God is jealous?

I thought jealousy was a *human* emotion. Why would a perfect being all majestic in power, creator of the universe, with the ability to wipe out humankind through a flood or something, be jealous? Huh? If God really were this jealous of people or the New York Yankees, then I had to conclude that God was petty, insecure, vengeful, selfish, and well, downright unpleasant. I mean jealousy is one of the most unappealing human qualities there is, right up there with pride and arrogance.

Lesson 4 – God told Abraham to have sex with a concubine. In other words, adultery was ok if God willed it.—Genesis 16:1-3

This story was a bit "R" rated for children in Vacation Bible School, but it was included at some point. We knew what adultery was because we had read the Ten Commandments (and I saw the movie). For some reason this story never mentioned that adultery might be involved because God seems to approve of this. At least Sarah, Abraham's wife, did.

The point of the story wasn't about sex anyhow. The story was meant to show how the Arab people came to be, through the lineage of Ishmael, the son of Hagar who was Abraham's concubine. These were people that were not part of God's promise to Abraham, so they were to be forever at odds with the Hebrews. The story really wasn't about sex or adultery at all, but to show that the Arabs are not God's people. Xenophobia justified.

Any reading of Bible stories from the Old Testament revealed that polygamy was common and not directly condemned by God. Solomon had quite a few wives and I thought that was just the perk of being a King. The misogyny of the Bible is very clear although not reserved just to God's people. Ancient societies and many today still practice polygamy. But the confusing question was, what is true biblical marriage? Reading the Old Testament and the New Testament made it difficult to figure out what the right pattern of marriage was supposed to be.

Lesson 5 – Lot wanted to give his daughters to the townsmen to be raped. Hey! Did anyone ask the girls?—Genesis 19

Of course, we learned this story so that we would all want to avoid a homosexual lifestyle. That seemed to be the key lesson that we were taught. But when we read the passage in Genesis 19:10 that said, *"Behold, I have two daughters who have not known man; let me bring them out to you and do to them as you please; only do nothing to these men, for they have come under the shelter of my roof."* I fixated on that passage.

To a kid my age, I wondered why Lot would give his daughters up to be raped and abused by these townsmen? To my immature mind, I concluded several things: men are more important than women, and by extension, sons must be of higher value than daughters. I also figured that raping a woman must be less evil than having gay sex.

Perhaps the biggest question I had about this awful passage of scripture was this. Did Lot ever even ask his daughters about this plan? I mean, what were these young girls thinking all this time whilst Lot was offering them up to be raped and God knows what else would happen? Did they get a say in this? Again, I learned quickly how to be a misogynist from this lesson.

Lesson 6 – God makes people do things against their will all the time. (Exodus 14) In other words, we really don't have free will.

This lesson seemed to come up every year. It is a popular one about the story of the Exodus, and how God hardened the hearts of the Egyptians. Why did God do that? I was always confused by that and the VBS teachers never really could answer it. I know that the Pharaoh was a bad guy, I mean, my picture of him was based on the stern-looking, arms-crossed Yul Brynner in the *Ten Commandments*.

It always bothered me that God didn't seem to give the Pharaoh a choice at all. If God made him to be mean and wanted to keep the Hebrews as slaves and then sent them out to the Red Sea to capture them again, why would God drown them all when it was God that caused him to do it in the first place? That just sounded so capricious. That is not a word I would have used as a kid, but looking back on it, seems appropriate now. Was God really that capricious?

If God were that capricious in the Old Testament, what if God were to harden my heart and cause me to do things that he would then later condemn me for doing? We were always taught that God is love, didn't God love the Pharaoh too? I never got this one as a kid. Still seems hard to understand if you take it literally.

Lesson 7 – God will destroy the false prophets with fire. (I Kings 18) In other words, all other religions are wrong.

This story wasn't as confusing or frightening as some of the others, in fact, we all thought this story was pretty cool. Elijah confronts the false prophets of Baal and they have a little contest to see which god would answer their petitions to send down fire for the animal sacrifice they had prepared. (There is that darned animal sacrifice again.)

I thought it was great how Elijah taunted the false prophets and made fun of their gods. After they failed to bring down fire on their sacrifices Elijah called on God and we knew what was going to happen. God sent down a consuming fire to burn the sacrifice. We could see this through our imaginations. But then Elijah took the false prophets down to the river and killed them there. Those bad guys had it coming, how dare they worship a false god.

The lesson I carried away from this is that God will not tolerate any deviation or any false religion. We were taught about all the false religions out there in our day, the Mormons, the Hare Krishnas, the Hindus, and even the Catholics. I figured someday they will all get their just judgment. But it began to instill a potent sense of intolerance for other faiths and religions.

I did wonder why God just didn't send down a fire and destroy them all today you know, maybe use Billy Graham like he did Elijah. But we were told God didn't do that sort of thing anymore for which I was grateful. But the message was still clear. Do not tolerate other faiths.

These are the lessons from Vacation Bible School and years of Sunday School as well, that I've had to unlearn and try and relearn a more reasoned and sensible view of life, the Bible and the whole nature of God. It does make me wonder just how much good these sorts of programs are actually doing in the minds of kids, but that is for parents to decide. Believe me kids internalize these stories in ways adults don't realize.

I'll close with a quote from one of my favorite writers that has helped me to see that there is another way to view the ancient texts; nonliteral, in their historic-cultural context, and metaphorically. The late Bishop John Shelby Spong of the Episcopal Church said in his book, *Biblical Literalism: A Gentile Heresy: A Journey into a New Christianity Through the Doorway of Matthew's Gospel:*

> "Then I realize, no, I am not dreaming, this is reality. People are actually reading the stories of a 5000 year-old ancient tribal theocracies and believing that they are literally the verbatim dictation of the creator of all existence. And because of that they are discriminating, denying science, and ignoring the environment. Just, wow!"[1]

I agree! Just, WOW!

SIX

WHAT TO DO ABOUT THE B-I-B-L-E?

The B-I-B-L-E
Yes, that's the book for me
I stand alone on the Word of God
The B-I-B-L-E.

WE SANG THIS JINGLE every Sunday morning in our Sunday School class and were taught to believe that the Bible was the inspired word of God through songs, lessons, and images. The Bible was vividly displayed at the front of the church sanctuary along with candles and other religious images. The message was clear, the Bible is to be revered if not worshiped as God's final word and message to humankind. Every Sunday when a section of the gospels was read in church we were required to stand. It was considered infallible, inerrant in every word and to be used with respect and reverence.

As a young person one of the greatest gifts you could receive was a red letter edition of the Bible with your name engraved at the bottom of the front cover. I received several. Bibles were given out for key events such as baptism, a birthday or a graduation. The *Gideons* gave us Bibles in elementary school year after year, something that has been discontinued. But, at any given point in time, I owned four or five Bibles at once.

More important than the awe and reverence built around the Bible was the way in which the Bible was used. Every preacher would say, *"the Bible says,"* and in Bible classes, it was common to hear, *"the Bible teaches us."* You can fill in the blanks. If the Bible says something is true, then it is true. It is the final authority that puts an end to any dispute or argument. It was the source of all authority. And if the Bible was silent about a topic, then "biblical principles" would suffice to provide guidance and an end to any alternate points of view.

Then there were the short easy-to-remember mantras about the Bible's authority that scholarly and well-educated pastors and teachers would say. Things like, "*The Bible says it, I believe it, and that settles it*" usually with reference to creation vs. evolution debates. Or you often hear, *"I'm just following what the Bible teaches"* after passing judgment on someone's looks, behavior or sexual orientation. I also heard this one many times growing up, *"Where the Bible speaks, we speak. Where the Bible is silent, we are silent."* Of course, this wasn't true. They spoke about things outside of the Bible all the time, but it did create a deference to the authority of the "Good Book" that was well ingrained by the time I was a teenager.

I read and studied the Bible continuously as a teenager and college student. I attended Bible studies and sometimes led them. I honed my skills as a teacher of the Bible and shared my knowledge and Biblical prowess in youth groups and coffee houses. I would have been called a "Bible-thumper" by many of my peers and that wouldn't have been too far off.

It was a short and easy step from believing the Bible to be the authoritative word of God to using it as a cudgel for bludgeoning the flock into obedience. I saw it happen and was quite willing to engage in such an offense myself.

Upon graduating from High School, I went to . . . wait for it . . . a . . . *Bible College*. There I learned some of the same lessons I had heard all through my indoctrination in church as a child, only with more scholarly sources that supported the theme that the Bible is literally true in all it says.

I went to Seminary to learn about how to promote Christian Education which was mostly about how to make the Bible the center of everything that is taught or how to think. And in turn as a teacher in a Christian Schools I taught not only history, but also Bible Classes that promoted the same sacred reverence and deference to the Bible. I passed along this same philosophy about the Bible that typical fundamentalist or evangelical churches today still espouse.

Did you notice what was missing in these descriptions of church life and experience? Less emphasis on Jesus and a continued, non-stop emphasis on the Bible. Certainly, we learned lessons about Jesus, but the church I attended spent way more time trying to convince us of the authority of the Bible. Jesus was secondary.

This has all changed for me. I no longer believe the Bible to be the literal-inerrant word of God. I can no longer hold the view that the Bible is the only source of truth and ethics. In the process I've undergone over that past 20 years, what does one do with the Bible? How do you deconstruct or re-evaluate a book that has been used as a basis for all philosophy and teaching for decades?

Evangelical churches and institutions make belief in the literal truth and inerrancy of the Bible a major component of faith and acceptance in those institutions. If you question or cast doubt on the Bible's veracity you are on a one-way street toward expulsion or "disfellowship" as it is called. This issue is a deal-breaker, so you don't go down this street unless you are ready to sacrifice a lot. Friends, often family, and certainly your Evangelical reputation are on the line.

How did I get there and what do I do with the Bible now? After deconstructing my faith and redefining it, what place do I give the Bible now? What I'll share next are the doubts and thought processes that I went through in changing my view of the Bible. Then I can share what I consider to be a better and perhaps healthier perspective on the Bible today.

Here are some of the reasons I ditched decades of teachings about the Bible. Even during those years as a "Bible-thumper" there were doubts, major doubts about what I was reading and teaching. Here are a few of the reasons for the shift in my view.

This is not meant to be a full theological discussion or dissertation on the Bible. This is more like a tour through my own mind and thought process which was based on much deeper study and reflection. I suggest each person needs to study and research this topic for themselves and reach their own conclusions. These are simply mine.

Other Sacred Books

In high school I was an avid reader and spent many hours in the school library reading mostly religious literature. I knew about other faiths and religions and was quite curious about them. I read other sacred books from other religions, and surprisingly, found much to admire in them. There were many common themes with the Bible in other ancient texts, which shouldn't be surprising, but it was of keen interest to me.

I'd been told that Christianity is the only way to God, and the Bible is God's only authoritative word. Why then were these other ancient texts considered sacred in other cultures? Why were "we" right and "they" wrong? Was it possible that God was speaking through those writers too? Why would wisdom be exclusive to one religion?

These questions ran through my brain but always seemed to run into the indoctrination I had received. No, the Bible is the only sacred word of God. Those other cultures must be mistaken. But these questions remained and lingered for a long time.

Historical Analysis of the Bible

As a history teacher I was always interested in the history of the Old and New Testament. Growing up I was given the impression that the Bible was one long, really long, book. Authorship, although admittedly by many people, were all unified by the work of the Holy Spirit to create a single, unified text from Genesis to Revelation.

We were never taught to think about the Bible as a list of 66 separate books, written by 40 or so separate individuals at different times in history each with a different context. Each book has very different authors with a particular purpose for writing, in a particular context and time period and for a specific audience. Understanding the setting of each book is important to seeing the reason why the imagery and language are used as they are. Most of the time the ancient imagery and language are not literal, but figurative. Attempting to make all the events in the Bible literally true reduces their meaning and impact.

I was led to believe that everything in the Bible was considered to be historically true or events that actually happened. For that to be true, you have to believe in the supernatural since so many of the events in the Bible defy physical laws as we know them. The parting Red Sea, Jonah in the belly of a whale, and the sun standing still in the sky are just a few of the supposed historical events that would require a supernatural being or God.

What I learned through the process of historical criticism is that though many events in the Bible are historical in nature, they are better interpreted in a cultural and metaphorical way. There are so many problems with the historical texts that I concluded that the Bible was never meant to be interpreted as historic literature and certainly not literal in every instance. The writers of the various books of the Bible are not writing historic accounts per se but interpreting events through the lens of Jehovah and their Jewish culture and trying to make a case that there is only one God. Modern historical scholarship has reduced the credibility and necessity of believing everything in the Bible is historically true. There is no need to argue such.

Scientific Errors Within the Bible

If the Bible were authored by God, then you would think the science within it would be correct. There are just too many inaccuracies scientifically to take this book as the final word on science. Here are some examples: earth is only 6,000 to 10,000 years old, there was a global flood, and the order of creation. There are many more, but I call these the mega-problems. Much of this inaccuracy stems from trying to interpret the Bible as a literal scientific text. If you leave behind that method of reading, then these stories become what they were likely intended to be, myths. These are myths that tell a story and create a narrative about the world, God's place in it and humankind's place in it. That makes these stories interesting and worth reading for their cultural content.

Let's take the big three one at a time and see the problems:

1) ***the earth is only 6,000 to 10,000 years old.*** Everything that we know for sure in science and radiometric dating places the earth at around 4.6 billion years old. Archeological evidence suggests that Homo Sapiens began migrating into North and South America at least 12,000 to 15,000 years ago and ice layers in Antarctica have been dated as far back as 800,000 years ago. There is no scientific evidence for a young earth.

2) ***there was a global flood.*** If a global flood occurred in the last several thousand years, it would leave a huge amount of observable evidence including geological deposits, changes in the distribution of species and a marked reduction in DNA diversity. Of course, no such evidence exists. There is more refutation to the idea of a global flood, but the lack of geologic deposits alone is enough.

3) ***order of creation.*** There are two creation accounts in the book of Genesis which do not agree. That is more of a contradiction. But the problem with the first Genesis account is scientific: on day one, God created light, but on day four he created the sun and the moon. If God then created plants on day three, how did photosynthesis take place? On the fifth day, water life was then created before land animals, which is correct scientifically. But birds were also created on day five which doesn't fit. Birds evolved long after land animals emerged. There is much more that can be pointed out but trying to fit a round peg into a square hole simply doesn't work. If God somehow dictated the words of the Bible, then why would he give false information about the order of creation? That seems to be a key thing. Even if the writer doesn't understand the biology and chemistry of creation at least God could have given him the right order.

Contradictions and Distortions Within the Bible

Depending on what you count as a contradiction or distortion there are many hundreds of them within the pages of the Bible. That should not be surprising or even disqualifying. If there were dozens of different writings over hundreds of years writing from their own cultural perspectives, I would be surprised not to find contradictions.

These contradictions are well documented in many articles and books. One of the more glaring examples shows the problem of contradictory passages. The issue is whether God loves everyone. Of course, the standard answer is yes God loves all humankind. John 3:16 is proof. But there is a problem when you juxtapose John 3:16 with another verse from Malachi 3:1, where the prophet says that "God hated Esau." Well in this case then, there is one exception apparently.

It goes further than one exception: God hates false witnesses and busybodies (Proverbs 6:16). God hates all workers of iniquity (Psalm 5:5). God hates wicked people and those that love violence (Hosea 9:15). What does this mean? Is God schizophrenic? Does God love everyone? Well, it depends.

If you are trying to defend the Bible as inerrant you will need to do pretzel-like contortions to make these verses fit.

Perhaps that isn't the goal. If the Bible was written by human beings with their own biases, concerns, goals, objectives, and wisdom to share, perhaps the contradictions are a natural result. And that's ok. It is freeing to relieve yourself of the need to protect the Bible from criticism.

Instead, read the text for what it is. Accept the flaws and contradictions because that is the nature of being human. It doesn't mean you have to reject the Bible and forget about it, but accept it for what it is, ancient wisdom literature written by flawed humans several thousand years ago.

Absurdity of Interpreting the Bible Literally

Reading the Bible literally and claiming inerrancy is a quest for certainty and security. People that want to defend biblical literalism above all other beliefs simply cannot live in a world of ambiguity and uncertainty. Some people need a solid theological place to hang their hat that doesn't change or move.

More insidious is perhaps the desire to use biblical literalism as a tool to prove that one's theological positions are correct on everything from a young earth to the virgin birth of Christ, to denying that gay marriage is legitimate. In order to be right all the time, biblical literalism, which is used selectively, is the tool.

John Shelby Spong, the late Bishop of the Episcopal Church, said in an interview not long before he died,

> "The literalization of the Gospels is not the result of the authors, it's the result of a generation 150 years after the birth of Jesus who didn't know the Jewish tradition so they couldn't see these connections. They didn't know, for example, that the feeding of the 5,000 was not a miracle. It was a retelling of Moses' manna in the wilderness story heightened and applied

> to Jesus. That's a very different perspective so the Jews never argued about whether Jesus really fed all those people with five loaves and two fish. But, if you see it as a familiar story in the Jewish tradition where the food supply is expanded in the Moses story, and in the stories of Elijah and Elisha, then you can retell it about Jesus and magnify it."[1]

Some of the absurdity of reading the Bible literally I've pointed out already. Some of the modern literal interpretations would most likely be a surprise to the authors of the text and would make it unrecognizable to them. In other words, the Bible wasn't written with the intent of being taken literally and much of the text indicates that. As Rachel Held Evans has said, everyone is a literalist until you bring up "gluttony."

Beyond that silly example which might be more true than not, there are multiple ways in which literal interpretations are just absurd. Don't eat shellfish (Leviticus 11); women should cover their heads in church (I Corinthians 11); don't call someone an idiot or you may burn in hell, (Matthew 5); slavery is justified (Ephesians 6:5); remarriage after divorce is adultery (Matthew 19:9); a disobedient and rebellious son should be stoned to death (Deuteronomy 21:18); adultery should result in the death penalty (Deuteronomy 22:22); if your eye causes you to sin, gouge it out (Matthew 18:9); and if your hand or foot causes you to sin, cut them off (Matthew 5:30).

These are a few of the more absurd statements that even the most ardent literalist doesn't seem to take seriously. And that is the point. Anyone that says they take the Bible literally only does so selectively. It is usually in relation to a pet rule, denominational creed, or dogma that they like to promote and inflict on other people or use to separate themselves from others as the "true church." And worse, biblical literalism has been used to promote patriarchal, homophobic, and anti-Semitic movements that bring real harm to people.

For me, I have rejected many prior beliefs about the Bible. I don't believe it is inspired as the only word of God or is inerrant or infallible. The text itself argues against such a position. But without that bedrock idea, then what are we left with? How do we view and use the Bible now?

As a recovering Evangelical the Bible still holds important meaning and significance. In fact, in some ways, the Bible takes on greater meaning and significance if we take away the literalization of it. I haven't just thrown my Bible collection out, but I have adjusted and reformed the way in which I use this ancient book. There are four reasons the Bible is still relevant to me. I'll explain each of these.

- To understand ancient society and history
- To gain wisdom and insight for living today
- Understand the depths of human nature both good and bad
- To gain insight into the universal nature of faith and its connection to all humans

Understand Ancient Society and History

Because I study and teach history the Bible is still an invaluable tool to peer back in time to the life and workings of ancient Jewish societies and other civilizations that were contemporary to it. In this sense the Bible is useful as a historical source even given its allegorical nature. Much can be learned about antecedents to our own civilization. Any person interested in understanding western culture and history will need a strong foundation and background in Biblical history.

Gaining Wisdom and Insight for Living Today

There is so much in the Bible that radiates wisdom and insight to how one should live their lives. From the book of Proverbs to the Psalms, the Prophets and the teachings of Jesus in the New Testament, the wisdom is timeless. Additionally, the beauty of these writings in lyric and prose is inspiring. I Corinthians 13, the love chapter is such an example of the soaring beauty of ancient texts.

A few examples are useful:

> "There is no fear in love, but perfect love casts out fear. For fear has to do with punishment, and he who fears is not perfected in love."—John 4:18

> "So we do not lose heart. Though our outer nature is wasting away, our inner nature is being renewed every day. For this slight momentary affliction is preparing for us an eternal weight of glory beyond all comparison, because we look not to the things that are seen but to the things that are unseen; for the things that are seen are transient, but the things that are unseen are eternal." — 2 Corinthians 4:16-18

> "A friend loves at all times, and a brother is born for adversity." — Proverbs 17:17

> "Let not loyalty and faithfulness forsake you; bind them about your neck, write them on the tablet of your heart. So you will find favor and good repute in the sight of God and man.." — Proverbs 3:3-4

> "With all lowliness and meekness, with patience, forbearing one another in love, eager to maintain the unity of the Spirit in the bond of peace." — Ephesians 4:2-3

> "Love is patient and kind; love is not jealous or boastful; it is not arrogant or rude. Love does not insist on its own way; it is not irritable or resentful; it does not rejoice at wrong, but rejoices in the right. Love bears all things, believes all things, hopes all things, endures all things." — I Corinthians 13:4-7

The beauty and wisdom of these verses are just a sampling of the inspiring narrative within the Bible. One does not have to be a literalist or an Evangelical to gain support, direction, and guidance from such verses.

Understand the Depths of Human Nature, Both Good and Bad

One aspect that I love and appreciate about the Bible is its raw, naked presentation of human nature. It doesn't always try to amplify the good and minimize the bad. Humans act and feel with real emotion and passion within the pages of the Bible. There are villains and crooks in the Bible both of whom act with courage or compassion at times. There are heroes in the Bible that despite their sacrifices and honor also act with selfishness and pettiness. The stories of King David are a great example of this type of flawed hero.

The Bible is a human book and I think that is the point of it. Despite all the hyperbole around its inspiration or inerrancy, there is so much more to learn by simply allowing the humanness of the characters to come alive. Think about the exuberance and passion of the disciple Peter and compare it to the dour and circumspect Thomas or even the more tortured soul of Judas. These are real individuals that reflect both the best and worst of human beings. How alike are we to them when we come into contact with the divine?

Consider the teachings of Jesus. His teachings turn everything about human nature on its head. It is counterintuitive in so many ways: *the first shall be last, blessed are the merciful, blessed are the peacemakers.* Jesus is calling us to a much higher plane of humanity and social interaction. Becoming completely and deeply human is the higher calling.

Insight Into the Universal Nature of Faith and Its Connection to All Humans

I believe the story being told in the Bible is one of expansiveness and inclusion. Again, the teachings of Jesus are key. *"The kingdom of heaven is in you; be one with each other as I and God are one; no greater love has any person than to lay their life down for a friend."* Faith in all its unspeakable and undefined facets connect us to each other and the divine that lives in each human being. Themes in the Bible connect us to each other whether we are Jewish, Roman, Samaritan, or black or white, male or female.

If we read the Bible as though it were inerrant and infallible, we spend most of our time defending, explaining, arguing and disputing the passages and what they mean. If we approach the Bible as an ancient book of wisdom, tragedy, human failings and victories, and most of all, a book of the universality of faith and consciousness, we can find our way to new heights of human discourse and interaction. The Bible along with all the other ancient sacred texts, and modern scientific understanding can together lead us to a new era of human cooperation and unity.

I think Father Richard Rohr says it well: "In our understanding of who God is, God becomes less violent, less punitive, more inclusive, less tribal–that to me is pretty obvious. And I think it's what we meant when we said that we read the scriptures in the light of Jesus."[2]

Amen!

PART TWO

FAITH & RACIAL JUSTICE: BECOMING ANTI-RACIST

SEVEN

A FUNNY THING HAPPENED

ON THE WAY TO A POST RACIAL SOCIETY IN AMERICA

This idea of a post-racial society was quite possibly the most sophisticated racist idea ever created. Because unlike previous racist ideas, that specifically told us how we should think about particular people of color . . . What post-racial ideas did was it said to us racism doesn't exist, racist policy doesn't exist, in the face of all of these racial inequities. And so then it caused us to say, OK, this inequity, like, the black unemployment rate being twice as high as the white unemployment rate, it can't exist because of racism. It must exist because there's something wrong with black workers.[1]

—**Ibram X. Kendi**, 2019

REMEMBER JUNE 17, 2015!

The idea of killing unarmed black people having a Bible study inside a church could have originated in only one of two ways. Either Dylann Storm

Roof, in his tortured deranged mind, gave birth to this idea out of thin air with no cultural influence or, he learned hate and violence from the culture around him and simply acted out on this idea to start a race war. I think the answer is obvious.

It took quite a while to put my thoughts and feelings into words concerning the racially motivated shooting at the Charleston Emmanuel AME church in South Carolina on that summer day in 2015. On one level, my heart broke for the families and friends of the victims that lost their lives. No amount of sympathy and sorrow will restore what they have lost. I know I feel a sense of grief and pain hundreds of miles away from Charleston, so I can only imagine the pain and sorrow that community experienced.

It was heartening to see the local response of people coming together of all races, prayer vigils, holding hands, weeping together, and calls for peace, forgiveness, and non-violence. That is a remarkable response in the face of such hatred and violence, and it speaks to the power of conscious spiritual strength and love. It is the only way an individual and the community will heal and restore itself. Of that I have no doubt. Hate will not and cannot win.

On another level, this is an event that also calls out for national mourning and reflection just as the murder of George Floyd called out for action. It speaks to our national character and aspirations and calls into doubt what we hope the United States is and will become.

Every white American needs to think deeply about this event and decide whether to contribute to the healing and building of a multi-racial society or continue to refuse to accept that the United States does indeed have a race problem.

Race is an ongoing issue, and our society has both overt and covert institutions, messages and systems designed to continue the historic segregation and bigotry that litters our history as a nation. Jon Stewart called it the "racial wallpaper" that constantly reminds people, both black and white, of our racial heritage and continued racial divide and teaches people to hate. It is the wallpaper of white supremacy.

A bit of historical context may help to put this event in 2015 in perspective. I'll use my own experience and observations from the past 50 years and from the perspective of a white-male, Protestant who grew up in a white community, went to a white school and a white church.

Right, what could a guy like me possibly have to say about race in America? Well, racial relations are a two-way street. White people need to walk a mile in someone else's shoes before making judgments and the healing can only come through reconciliation. Reconciliation can only happen when both parties realize there is a breach or breakdown of a relationship.

There are many white males that don't even recognize or admit that there is a problem. I'm not sure how much more evidence one needs than the nine dead bodies in the church in South Carolina to dispel this notion that somehow, we live in a post-racial society. Evidence is all around.

I came of age in 1963. Born in 1955, the year that Rosa Parks started a major civil rights movement by refusing to give up her bus seat to a white person, the fight for civil rights was a constant thread throughout my childhood and teen years. I remember the March on Washington, and Dr. King's speech in front of thousands of people. I saw the newsreels of police brutality in places like Montgomery and Selma. I knew intuitively that something was desperately wrong.

I remember some of the conversations I heard among grandparents and family members that were extremely bigoted and derogatory toward black people and wondered why they were so angry at them. And then in school, I heard racist jokes about blacks and other ethnic groups from teachers. Yes, sadly from teachers.

Then there were race riots all over the country in the 1960's, even as close to home as a few neighborhoods over from where I lived. It was a violent time, and I grew to realize that anytime the status quo is challenged or changed, hatred and bigotry emerged.

I witnessed the Civil Rights Act of 1964, the Voting Rights Act of 1965 and the Equal Opportunity Protection laws of the late 60's come into being.

What was dying was the 100-year-old Jim Crow system that had created two societies, one black and one white.

Jim Crow was as much about retaining white privilege as it was about ensuring a subservient status for Black people. And though the legal framework for Jim Crow was dismantled by legislation at that time, the cultural vestiges of that system continued to exist, and still do today. Jim Crow of the heart is alive and well. No one changed the wallpaper.

This is what I think many people today miss in the aftermath of the election of the first black president Barack Obama. I have heard over and over that race is no longer an issue and we now live in a post-racial society and bigotry is a thing of the past. We have laws to forbid discrimination. But what we haven't changed is the wallpaper of racism and hatred. Much of this cannot be legislated out of existence but can come only through willing change, hard work, acceptance of the problem, and reconciliation.

So, what is that "wallpaper" of racism that still exists? It isn't hard to see if you are looking. Here are some of the more salient examples.

White privilege is still part of our society and system. I'm not suggesting that this is even an overt system though in some places it is. This is a system that gives whites an advantage by virtue of where they are born, the color of their skin, and a system that provides more open doors and opportunities for whites than it does for blacks.

Personal examples may help. I'll start with law enforcement. I grew up trusting the police. I never, not one time ever thought that the police were out to hurt or harm me in any way. In fact, it was quite the opposite. I saw the police in my community as positive role models and even friends.

In a recent Gallup Poll, it was clear that Black people, especially young Black males, do not have the same attitude toward the police.[2] This has played out over and over in the past few years in places like Ferguson, New York, Cleveland, and Baltimore, but it is widespread.

As a young white man, I walked the streets never fearing the police, even though I probably should have been arrested a few times. White privilege allowed me to have immunity from concern, and even if I had been arrested, I would not have feared mistreatment.

To the contrary, Robert Brame, South Carolina Professor of criminology and author of a major study published in 2014 said, "A problem is that many males – especially black males – are navigating the transition from youth to adulthood with the baggage and difficulties from contact with the criminal justice system."[3]

In other words, the criminal justice system is part of the wallpaper of racism in many parts of our country. And incarceration rates clearly show the propensity for Black people to be arrested and imprisoned more often than whites.

White privilege also shows itself in our school systems. I grew up in a community where school attendance was mandatory and expected. Dropping out was not an option. I was taught that by working hard and doing well in school I could advance. And I took advantage of this opportunity. It was there. Schools were adequately funded, and I had good teachers and just about any opportunity that I would want to find.

It was a stark reality to find out that these conditions are not the same everywhere. If I had been born into a different community under a different zip code, these same opportunities and funding would not have been there. Some students, particularly those in urban neighborhoods with large minorities are underfunded, have dropout rates many times as high as other communities and it isn't at all clear that hard work and effort will lead to success. I found this out first-hand when I started my teaching career in a large urban school system in an underserved neighborhood where poverty rates were nearly 90%.

This brings up another piece of the wallpaper that might be the most insidious of all: housing discrimination. It is clear historically that the neighborhoods that are ethnically defined were the deliberate result of unfair housing practices such as "blockbusting", "restrictive covenants," "redlining" and other unfair housing practices that existed in the 20th Century. Blacks were relegated to poor and declining communities with lower property values on purpose. These communities experienced not only poor schools but fewer job opportunities, and fewer services to improve their communities.

Although these practices were made illegal by the 1968 Fair Housing Act, many cities and towns continued to practice them in more covert ways. Courts were reluctant to prosecute these practices and few remedies were enacted to enforce fair practices.

What is startling about this chapter of American racial history is that it was deliberately enacted at the federal, state, and local level by government authority. The vestiges of these practices are still felt and seen by millions of American citizens. It is a key component of the American racial wallpaper today.

Some more wallpaper? White churches in America have generally done little to bridge the racial divide. Beyond the overt "Christian Identity" movement, which is considered a terrorist organization, there is still a Jim Crow of the heart mentality within many churches.

It is no secret that throughout American history preachers and churches have deliberately used the Bible to justify everything from slavery to segregation and white supremacy. But in the modern era, racism is still as much a part of the wallpaper but simply in different patterns.

Athena Butler in her book, "*White Evangelical Racism: The Politics of Morality*" makes a clear and unequivocal statement about Evangelical racist practices when she says,

> It is racism that binds and blinds many white American Evangelicals to the vilification of Muslims, Latinos, and African Americans. It is racism that impels many Evangelicals to oppose immigration and turn a blind eye to children in cages at the border. It is racism that fuels Evangelical Islamophobia. It was evangelical acceptance of biblically sanctioned racism that motivated believers to separate and sell families during

> slavery and march with the Klan. Racist Evangelicals shielded cross burners, protected church burners, and participated in lynchings. Racism is a feature, not a bug, of American Evangelicalism.[4]

For further example, Evangelicals, especially in the south, have created institutions to counter court ordered desegregation within schools. The Christian School movement which originated in the early 1950s in reaction to *Brown vs. Board of Education*, created a network of Segregation Academies that gave an outlet to white parents that did not want their children to associate with black children. Many Christian Colleges were established for the same reason. These schools have flourished and have tuition rates that bar poor black families from attending.

It is also important to note that the "Religious Right" founded by Jerry Falwell, Paul Weyrich and others, was a direct reaction to school desegregation policies that prompted many white evangelicals to open "segregation academies."

Although Bob Jones Jr., the founder of the school bearing his name, argued that racial segregation was mandated by the Bible, Falwell and Weyrich quickly sought to shift the grounds of the debate, framing their opposition in terms of religious freedom rather than in defense of racial segregation. But make no mistake, segregation was the goal.

Add to this white Evangelical support for Donald Trump in the 2016 election and since. Although surprising to many, this overwhelming support was expected within the Black Community. They were not shocked at the white religious community's support for a man who at one time refused to rent apartments to blacks in New York and who engendered support from groups like the KKK, and then appointed a White Nationalist to the office of Sr. White House Advisor. White privilege is alive and well in Trump's America and within the Evangelical voter bloc that he commands.

Butler makes this observation in her book about Evangelical support for Donald Trump in 2016.

> Evangelicals' embrace of an unrepentant racist solidified the place of racism in the history of American Evangelicalism. More than that, their embrace tore the covers off the anti-Black racism that had existed since the nineteenth century.[5]

The effect of these types of white privilege and unfair systemic practices toward Black people is to give our children different starting lines from birth depending on their zip code. If it were an actual foot race it would be like giving the white kids a starting line a hundred yards further ahead on the track than the black kids. It isn't hard for the black kids to realize that they are starting out with a disadvantage and the system is rigged.

As for me, no one ever sat down and said to me, "you are white, and you have more privileges than people of color...here is how it works..." No, it was simply part of the culture and social system into which I was born, unspoken, and unacknowledged, but present nonetheless.

The wallpaper of racism in the U.S. has an even more overt face. That of hate groups and white supremacists. And this is apparently where our thug Mr. Roof, was awash with influence. (I use the term thug deliberately in contrast to how the media described Roof). Although it isn't clear if Roof was a member of any of the 19 different white supremacist groups that exist in South Carolina, clearly, he had swallowed their message of hatred and bigotry.

Lest we blame South Carolina alone, these hate groups exist in every state of the Union including here in my home state, Iowa. You know, that "nice" state. And the patches that Roof was wearing on his jacket that included the Apartheid era flag of South Africa, has been a common part of many white supremacy rallies not only in the U.S., but in other countries as well. Roof did not have a sudden epiphany to go out and shoot Black people for no reason. The subculture of white supremacy had taught him to hate black people and to seek a race war.

Racism is a learned behavior and attitude. White Americans should not feel guilty for being white. But when the wallpaper of our culture clearly imprints racism on our society as it does then white Americans have a responsibility to change it. That process begins by recognizing and accepting that racism does indeed exist, and white privilege is part of our system.

What it takes to recognize this I believe, is humility, self-awareness and a desire to learn about systemic racism. What black people see as part of "being black in America" every day, I need to hear, listen, and learn about from their experience and not try and rationalize or debate it away. It exists despite my blindness or ignorance of it.

In addition to changing policy and practices within our schools, real estate industry, law enforcement, churches and other social institutions, change can come through spiritual renewal. By this I don't mean imposing Christianity or any other faith on our society. What I mean is that we would all do well to follow the example of the relatives and friends of the deceased in South Carolina and seek forgiveness and reconciliation. That is a personal spiritual exercise that requires more strength than anyone can ever imagine. But I believe this is where the pathway to a truly post-racial society must begin.

EIGHT

FREEDOM IS CONNECTED!

Although the importance of celebrating Juneteenth might be evident to Black folks, it should be every bit as important to those of us who are White because the liberation of Black people is the only hope for our own. The literal chains that bound Black bodies always, metaphorically, bound us as well: to a mindset of human inequality, the perpetuation of unspeakable horror, and the numbing of one's conscience necessary to make that horror acceptable.[1]

—Tim Wise, Antiracism Educator

THE HORRIBLE AND BRUTAL war in Ukraine shows us that freedom for all humans is connected. A threat to freedom in Ukraine is a threat to freedom in the United States and all other freedom loving countries.

It should also reinforce the fact that within American society the freedom of one group is connected to the freedom of all groups. This explains why white Americans need to recognize, commemorate, and celebrate Juneteenth.

June 19 is ***Juneteenth*** day for Black American citizens. I am embarrassed to admit that I only learned of this holiday a few years ago after a long career teaching history. I wish now that I could go back and reteach about this holiday to my students right alongside other major civic holidays like July 4, Memorial Day, Labor Day, and Veteran's Day. Juneteenth is just as important.

Growing up in an Evangelical church, Juneteenth was never observed or emphasized. Now, I need to ask, why? Our church was all white, and so July 4 was a holiday that our church regularly celebrated and even had special "freedom" services. American flags were displayed throughout the sanctuary and patriotic songs were sung.

We celebrated freedom for white people but never was it ever mentioned that Black Americans weren't included in the original proclamation of that freedom. In hindsight this was a major oversight. Was it on purpose, or due to ignorance?

If the "good news" meant we should celebrate our political freedom, then extending that political freedom to Blacks should be part of the celebration. Empathy here was sorely lacking.

Just because we were a primarily white church, itself a disconcerting phenomenon, it doesn't absolve us. Slavery, hatred, violence, and segregation were all products of white attitudes and actions. It isn't up to Black people to change white people's attitudes. White people have to do that for themselves. It may not be immediately apparent to white people, but racial hatred and enmity enslaves white people as much as physical slavery enslaved Black people. It is a slavery of the soul and conscience.

Here are a few observations about why Juneteenth is a day for all Americans to observe and celebrate, including white Americans.

June 19, 1865 was the day shortly after the Civil War was over, when Federal troops finally reached the last plantation in Texas where blacks were still enslaved and delivered the message that they were now free. It is perhaps one of the most important holidays for our black citizens in the US.

The question I would like to address is why should an overwhelmingly white community like the one in Iowa where I live, or white Americans in general, care about this or even celebrate this day?

It will start by stating and repeating this phrase:

"until everybody is free, there ain't nobody free."

This is a day for all of us to rejoice in the liberation of enslaved people from the cruel institution that had abused them for hundreds of years. Because,

"until everybody is free, there ain't nobody free."

Understand this! Slave owners were not free . . . and Americans that tolerated slavery or were apathetic about it, were not free. ***Slavery enslaved the enslaver*** in a web of hatred and distortion of the human soul. Hatred and bigotry are a cruel slave master of the soul because it distorted and denied basic humanity.

At the heart of this idea is the observable reality that we are all connected to one another. This is an important spiritual truth. Your well-being is connected to my well-being, and your prosperity is connected to my prosperity.

As much as we want to believe in the myth and ideal of rugged individualism, the reality is, we all are in this thing called *society*, together. We sink or swim, together.

My freedom is connected to everyone else's freedom. And that is why white Americans and especially white Christians need to celebrate this holiday. The freedom of enslaved black people is connected to the core of everyone's freedom. Because, if Black people can be enslaved and mistreated, anyone can be enslaved and mistreated. If Asians can be discriminated against and hated, then everyone can be discriminated against and hated. Because,

"until everybody is free, there ain't nobody free." *Get it?*

Now this connection goes even deeper than just what happened in 1865. Bigotry and hatred did not end on June 19, 1865. We are all aware of the Jim Crow era of discrimination and segregation. The lynching and attacks against people of color in that era damaged all of us because we are connected to each other. The white people that engaged in systematic slavery, and later, violence and intimidation against freed blacks were the ones damaged and in fact they were the ones enslaved to their own hatred. Slavery and racism might have been a physical thing that you can see, but the perpetrators of that violence were also enslaved. Their souls were dead to the humanity and connectedness of all humans. Because,

"until everybody is free, there ain't nobody free."

Not only are we all connected to one another today. History teaches us that we are connected to the past in ways we may not be aware. I'll share with you a personal story. It was a few years ago as I was studying my family history, that I discovered that my great-grandfather, James Franklin Henderson joined the Iowa Ku Klux Klan in the early 1900's.

Yes, there was indeed an Iowa KKK. He was born in 1859 and grew up in the post-Civil War era and was fashioned and conditioned by the racial hatred of that time and unfortunately gave in to that conditioning. This was only three generations ago. He died in 1937. I was born just a few years later in 1955, so you can see I am connected to my great-grandfather and his legacy of hatred. Each generation shapes the next one.

The good part of the story was that my grandfather, Erwin Henderson, disapproved of his father's activities, and would do things to sabotage his efforts, like hide his white sheet, and refuse to drive his father to the meetings. He ended up having to walk six miles to meet up with his KKK buddies.

I'm connected to my Grandfather too, and his legacy lives in me. The point is our souls are shaped by the past and our connection to people and events that either damage our souls or heal our souls. It either damages the soul of the nation or heals it.

What does this matter today? The damage done, both physically and spiritually, due to the institution of slavery and cruel Jim Crow era that followed has left a terrible legacy that exists today. We are all still connected to each other and to those past events. And when structural bias and racism continue to exist as we see now in housing, law enforcement, employment, health care, education, religion, government, and virtually every institution in our society; then we are all of us, still enslaved, both white and black. Because,

"until everybody is free, there ain't nobody free."

This brings us back to *Juneteenth*, and the reasons why all Americans need to recognize and celebrate this holiday. When white people can sincerely celebrate the freedom of blacks, it sets us free too, in our souls. When white people can reach out and accept the reality of the legacy of slavery and Jim Crow which still exist today, it will free our souls. And it will help to begin to heal the soul of our nation.

Celebrating this day along with our black brothers and sisters, and our Latino brothers and sisters, our native American brothers and sisters, and our Asian brothers and sisters will release all of us from the slavery of the soul and begin to heal us from the unconscious hatred that has been instilled in us for centuries, because we are all connected to each other. It will help to heal our country that is aching and writhing in the pain of unconscious racism. Because,

"until everybody is free, there ain't nobody free."

NINE

SIX THINGS WHITE PEOPLE SHOULD STOP SAYING

Still, here's the truth: You have not seen outrage until you have seen the face of a white person being called a racist. You would think seeing the image of Emmett Till's mutilated corpse in an open casket in 1955 or Michael Brown's body lying dead in a Missouri street in 2014 would evoke extreme shock and horror. But, actually, white people get the most worked up when they or someone they know have been labeled a racist. This kind of outrage comes because people see racism as a relic of the past. To them, racists are Klan members or old relatives to be tolerated over the holidays. How can anyone these days possibly be racist?[1]

—**Linda Chavers**, Harvard University

White people say the darndest things to keep from being called a racist. It is the ultimate insult and is to be avoided at all costs.

I get it, it is an emotional issue, and everyone wants to believe they are a good person. Especially white people; and especially white Christians.

In the wake of *Black Lives Matter*, police violence against black men, and the Capitol attack by groups of white supremacists, there is heightened awareness of racial injustice, and it is not acceptable in polite society to be considered a racist or to make racist comments.

To be considered a good white person, white people have engaged in language that on the surface doesn't seem racist and is in fact designed to create distance from racist attitudes and language. The problem with these statements, as well intended as they may be, is that they perpetuate racism and hide the systemic nature of it.

Christians in particular want to paint racism as a product of individual action or attitude and categorize racism as an individual sin. The six statements that I'll address obfuscate the structural nature of racism. This makes the situation worse. You will hear these phrases repeated over and over. It is as predictable as the sun rising each morning. And it is like a game. The game is to run and hide every time the word "racist" is used.

Picture in your mind a level field and everyone is playing a game on this field. Then all of a sudden someone on the other team shouts the word...RACISM! Immediately all the white people run around behind a fortified wall of defense on the sideline. That wall is made up of these retorts and defensive phrases. They stand behind the wall of these words and utter them many times without even being asked, as if to tempt the other team to try and touch them. They are protected. Safe! It is an automatic response that is designed to alleviate them of guilt and deflect the awful label of "racist."

The fallacy surrounding these phrases is that white people use them to try to absolve themselves of racist intent but give no thought to the impact the words have on people of color (POC). These phrases are defensive moves designed to assure everyone that they have no racist intent or motives. The impact of these words are harmful and contribute to racial problems as opposed to dismantling the white supremacist culture in which we live. These phrases perpetuate that culture.

Another way to say it is this. When white people use these phrases, they care more about being seen as a good person than the impact that racism actually has on persons of color. It indirectly re-centers the focus of the conservation on white people's feelings as opposed to the impact of racism on the feelings of people of color. White people care more about how they are perceived rather than how black people are treated.

It is likely that white people that use these six phrases have never asked a POC how they perceive these words. That would be the hard work of becoming antiracist. And frankly anyone that wants to engage in activist work and antiracism will need to start by examining their own mental models, paradigms, language, and past socialization. It will take much self-examination, reflection, and self-education to learn just what is the true impact of these phrases.

90% of the work of antiracism is the deconstruction of one's own racist socialization and unconscious bias. But it is much easier to just use these phrases to declare to everyone that you are a "non-racist." That takes no work, no thought, and no effort. And the only person you are fooling is yourself.

What are these phrases? Let's take a look at them one by one and break them down from the filter of the impact of these words on people of color, not just their intent for white people.

Here is the first phrase that white people need to stop saying:

"I don't see color I only judge people by what they do."

Let's break this down by using a different filter. The white filter is, "I'm a good person because I judge people according to the content of their character, not the color of their skin." It is the ultimate Martin Luther King Jr. card. Look at how noble I am because I quote MLK. But if we apply a person of color filter here is what it sounds like:

> I don't acknowledge your experience as a person of color. I don't see that you are four more times likely to be pulled over by the police than I. I don't see that you need to submit 10 resumes for every one of mine because people with a name like yours get passed over automatically. I don't acknowledge that people like you are dying at a much higher rate due to COVID because of unequal access to good jobs and health care. I don't see that the mass incarceration of black men in this country is about 10 times the proportion of the population of black people. I don't see that you are stalked and profiled in stores by clerks because of your skin color, and more often accused of theft. Yep . . . I don't see your experience.

It is gaslighting people of color in a way that shows you are not to be trusted as an ally. You are so worried about your precious reputation that you refuse to understand that the experience of a person of color is very different than yours, and it is because of their skin color. To tell people that you don't see color is to refuse to "walk a mile in their shoes."

But the reality is you *do* see color. You can't help it. It is there and because of how our culture has evolved, color does make a difference. Your unconscious biases are still there. They may not be visible or conscious to you, but they are there. Your statement that you don't see color only means you are woefully lacking in self-awareness which is another reason you can't be trusted.

Let's go on to the next phrase that white people need to stop saying:

"I was raised to love everyone equally."

No . . . no, you weren't. This is another defensive phrase to create distance between you and the "R" word . . . racist. Without doubt I'm sure your parents were great people and taught you well. But let's just run through a little checklist called the "socialization checklist."

How many shows did you watch on television as you were growing up that had a non-white nuanced, multi-layered complex character as the protagonist? (come on, man, even Tarzan was a white guy)

Who wrote the history textbooks that you read in school that taught history from a white point of view, downplaying the role of slavery, and painting a picture of all things in white culture are good and patriotic?

How many books in general did you have in your house or at school that were written by non-white authors?

How many times did your parents talk to you about race and racial injustice and explain to you why blacks and Hispanics make cents on the dollar compared to white people in our society?

Who explained to you how "redlining" neighborhoods in most American cities led to a lack of generational wealth being passed on through increasing home values?

Was there ever a time when you couldn't be around people of your own race (white) as opposed to being a minority in a group?

There are always a few exceptions to the rule, but the rule is still the rule. The point here is that no one, and I mean no one gets socialized in the United States without having racial stereotypes and attitudes imprinted on your mind and your soul. Whiteness is the preferred color even for children by the time they are 3 or 4 years old. Studies have borne this out time after time.

So...no you were not raised to love everyone the same. You were raised with biases that are now unconscious and buried in your psyche. But it is a nice sentiment designed to let white people off the hook of a white supremacist society. But it isn't true.

How about this one . . .

"I have Black friends so I can't possibly be racist."

This statement is a dead giveaway. When anyone says this, I want you to think of this analogy. I hope it will imprint on your mind.

Remember in the Middle East wars when terrorists would fight against American forces there? Many times, the terrorists would use human shields, innocent people many of which were women and children, to protect them from incoming strikes. They knew American forces might not strike them if they had human shields.

That's what this statement is. It is an attempt to use people of color as a shield against the incoming accusation of being racist. They believe that physical proximity to people of color absolves them from all the unconscious bias that they hold. They believe that because they have a black friend or co-worker, or even a person of color to whom they are married, it absolves them from all the socialization of their lifetime.

This statement does not in any way put the needs of people of color first. Just like the terrorist, white people want to use them to protect themselves. And people of color know it. So as soon as you say this, understand that you are only fooling yourself because people of color know what you are doing. You are not valuing them; you are putting your reputation first and using them as human shields to do so. It is a despicable statement to make.

Here is another one....

"Racism no longer exists, get over it, it happened a long time ago."

White people need to stop saying this. It is like the phrase, "I don't see color." It is a complete denial of reality. It is gaslighting once again by trying to paint reality for people of color different than it is.

If racism no longer existed, then George Floyd would still be alive, along with hundreds of other black people who have been killed for no other reason than they are black. If racism no longer exists, then the Capitol would not have been overrun by white supremacist groups carrying Confederate battle flags or wearing "Camp Auschwitz" t-shirts. And if racism no longer exists then blacks would make equal amounts of pay for equal jobs. Wealth inequality would be declining, not increasing.

Using the filter of Black people's eyes this phrase is particularly insidious because the reality of being black in America today is so much predicated on a racist system. And Black people understand the true intent of this phrase.

Every black person knows that the corollary to this statement is, "the only reason there is racism is because you talk about it." It reverses the guilt for a racist system. It's black people's fault for bringing this up. "We wouldn't have these problems if you just kept your mouths shut."

It's gaslighting . . . calling day night and night day. But ultimately the white person gets to say, "look how good and morally upright I am because I said racism doesn't exist. You're the bad person for bringing it up." Of these six phrases I list here, this one may be the most overtly racist one.

On to the next . . .

"I don't have white privilege because I've struggled in my life a lot"

Well, congratulations, you have joined the human race! Most people have struggled in their lives, but white people never had to struggle because of the color of their skin.

This statement represents white privilege more than anything I've ever heard. You are given a head start in the race at birth as a white person, but you just don't know it nor acknowledge it. And even if you were only born on first base, black people haven't even been able to come to plate yet.

I think white people that say this are probably sincere, but they are also sincerely short sighted. This statement, "white privilege" triggers white people a great deal. I've seen it first-hand.

White people like to believe they have struggled against all odds to earn and get what they have. No hand-outs . . . no charity. And they believe that what Black people are after is welfare, a free handout that they think is digging into their pockets.

The implied message from white people is that if you think I have privilege then "you need to just get a job and earn your own way, like I did." The real message is, "you are lazy, and I'm not . . . aren't I a good person?" Again, it is about making sure no one thinks I'm a bad person.

Here's what is true. Every white person born in the United States regardless of their circumstance, good or bad, rich, or poor, never had to deal with the obstacle and barrier of being black in this society. Many white people are born poor and in horrible circumstances. But they did not have the added burden of being black at the same time.

You were given handouts as a white person, but you didn't know it because it is built into the system. You were given privileges that no one ever explained to you. You never had to worry about being killed by the police if you were pulled over, and you never had to worry about walking down the street while white.

White privilege is the "knapsack of unearned favors" that society gives to you throughout your life. Peggy McIntosh first introduced this term to us in 1989, but whites have been privileged in our society for over 400 years.

As a white male of 60+ years, I have experienced those unearned favors time after time. I don't feel guilty for it because no one ever explained it to me. But now that I understand it, I feel responsible to share the privilege. It isn't about taking anything away from anyone...it is about sharing the unearned favors with people of color. Is there any reason they shouldn't have the same consideration as I?

Here is the last thing in my list that white people should stop saying:

"You don't know me so you can't say I am racist"

Yada, Yada, Yada! Yep, you're right. I don't know you. But I do know this...you watched the same television shows as I, and read the same textbooks that I did, and understood from an early age that being white had more value and honor than being black. You learned that white people were responsible for the success of this nation just as I did, and you were told that black people were less intelligent and able as white people.

I know that we all came from the same heritage of black discrimination and Jim Crow segregation regardless of what part of the country you lived in. So, spare me your self-serving rhetoric. I don't know you personally, but I know where you came from...and what values you were raised with.

Same as mine.

The difference is this, I'm willing to admit where I came from and what I learned and what I need to unlearn. I understand that I was born on second base, but I didn't hit a double. I know that throughout my life I never had to contend with being black while working my way through school and establishing my career. I had a hand up . . . even if I didn't ask for it. It was there, and I took it. I don't feel guilt for it, but I do feel responsible to extend the same privileges that I was afforded to everyone regardless of their skin color (which I see clearly) or their religion, or nationality. I have white privilege in a racist society. My job now is to dismantle racism, extend the privilege to everyone, and share my unearned handouts.

White privilege often shows up as a benefit of the doubt. I can walk out of the store without a receipt because I get the benefit of the doubt. I can drive a nice car without being pulled over and questioned about why I have a nice car, because I get the benefit of the doubt. I can go to a good college and never be questioned about how I got there because I get the benefit of the doubt. Black people never get these fringe benefits of the doubt. It's our job to extend the same privileges and benefits that white people have taken for granted for generations.

Are you willing to join me? Let's become anti-racists together, not just non-racists.

TEN

BECOMING ANTI-RACIST

Will racism ever be completely eliminated? Perhaps not; racism has its roots in human pride and sin, and these will never be completely erased until Christ comes again. But that shouldn't keep us from reaching out and trying to eliminate the barriers that divide us. Yes, laws have a place—but most of all, our hearts need to be changed, and only God can do that. And He will, as we open our hearts and lives to Christ's transforming love.[1]

—**Billy Graham**, 2005

Billy Graham's comment in 2005 toward the end of his life shows the internal conflict that he along with all Evangelical Christianity feels when it comes to the issue of race and racism. During the Civil Rights years which came at the height of his evangelistic career, Graham was quietly supportive of equal rights and equal treatment for blacks but never aggressively supportive nor took radical action. He did not join with Dr. Martin Luther King, a fellow pastor, in various marches for equality. He didn't join King on the steps of the Lincoln Memorial in 1963, and in fact criticized King's method of nonviolent civil disobedience.

Graham's rationalization for his tepid support of civil rights for blacks was rooted in a theological view of racism as a personal sin. He said, "racism has its roots in human pride and sin." His solution for the problem was a personal one. Wait for the return of Jesus and in the meantime, convert as many people to Christ as possible. For Graham, legal and social progress on the issue of race was predicated on a spiritual conversion in an Evangelical way. For Graham and other Evangelicals, combatting racism was not the priority, personal salvation was.

While this might have seemed like a logical answer, this view had many consequences which may not have been intended. There are three unintended consequences to the "Graham doctrine."

First, viewing racism as a personal sin blinded Evangelicals to the systemic and structural nature of racism that existed even within their own churches. It certainly exists in social, economic, and political arenas, but if racism is primarily a sin of the heart according to Christians, then it isn't structural. You can ignore the obvious inequities that exist within your own institutions.

As an Evangelical I accepted this view for many years. While I might have been the first one to decry racism and segregation because I accepted the assumption that it was personal sin, I was able to ignore taking any real action to end racism or dismantle a racist system because the goal was to win converts to Christ and then changed hearts would take care of racism all on its own. But this assumption leads to a second problem with this theology. It's a big problem.

Second, even many who are "born again" Christians are racists. This has been true in every generation of American history. Being born again is a guarantee of nothing when it comes to racist attitudes or actions even if you see it as a sin.

Historically, there has been a connection between racism and religion. In the 19th century, slaveholders and their sympathizers defended slavery by pointing to its presence in the Bible as evidence that it fit within God's plan for the social order. They also interpreted biblical stories like those about

Cain and Abel and the supposed "curse of Ham" as proof that God had made "Negroes" to be slaves.

During and after the years of Reconstruction, white Southerners and the Northerners who wanted to reestablish social and economic ties with them updated these older proslavery theologies to support an emerging Jim Crow establishment of racial segregation and discrimination.

Preachers, along with many others, developed a segregationist folk theology that defended the newly constructed Southern racial order as divinely ordained. God had created the races separate and did not intend for them to mix. This was common preaching in southern pulpits until even the 1960's.

In the 20th-century segregationists argued that the civil rights movement was trying to impose an anti-Christian, even communistic ideology that would destroy the Christian racial order of the South. *"Brown vs. Board of Education"* was interpreted this way as a threat to God's divine order.

According to segregationist interpretations of the Bible, black people were inferior to white people, cursed by God and naturally suited to second class status. Requiring white employers to hire black people or mixing white kids with black kids in school would violate these sincerely held religious convictions and threaten once again to destroy the settled racial order of the nation. So in the name of religious freedom, white Christian racists justified segregation, white supremacy and continued discrimination.

Being a "born-again" Christian might mean that you inherited an ingrained white supremacist point of view. Being a white Christian was associated with being a good American. Anything less was "un-American." Graham's assumption that once more people become born again then racism will take care of itself was just wrong, but it led to a third problem.

The third problem with viewing racism strictly as a personal sin or action is that it gives permission to do nothing about systemic racial injustice. In the reasoning of many white Protestants, white dominance was not the consequence of a political and economic arrangement, but the will of God – the way things are supposed to be. As Kelly Baker, author of "*The Gospel*

According to the Klan," states: "Even liberal Protestant churches supported white supremacy. That seemed the natural order of things. Just as people used biblical texts to support slavery."[2]

Billy Graham's theology taught that racism was simply part of the natural fallen order until Christ returned. If this were true, then hundreds of thousands of Evangelicals had permission to do nothing.

At most, Evangelicals, including Graham, supported a "gradualist" approach to changing the racist society. But a gradualist approach was simply another way of saying, let's kick the can down the road and deal with it another day, or even in another generation.

Graham gave a whole generation of Evangelicals permission to sit on the sidelines and in fact to support the status quo. You could see it clearly as private Christian academies opened all over the country, allowing white Christians to avoid sending their children to the newly integrated public schools.

In the 1970s, the IRS moved to revoke the tax-exempt status of Bob Jones University because of its racially segregated campus. As historian Randall Balmer described, the new religious right began to mobilize in the 1970s specifically against this IRS action. Opposition to abortion was secondary to this issue.

With the fusion of right-wing extreme politics with the Evangelical movement in the 1970's and beyond, the momentum of white supremacy associated with religion in America has only moved into high gear. We see the fruition of that unholy alliance in the support of Donald Trump overwhelmingly by Evangelicals and the emerging white nationalist movement that he encouraged. White Christians are consistently more likely than whites who are religiously unaffiliated to deny the existence of structural racism.

Consider these recent polling numbers conducted by the "*Public Religion Research Institute*" in 2018. They found that white Christians, including evangelical Protestants, mainline Protestants and Catholics, are nearly twice as likely as religiously unaffiliated whites to say the killings of Black men by police are isolated incidents rather than part of a pattern of how police treat African Americans.[3]

White Christians are about 30 percentage points more likely to say monuments to Confederate soldiers are symbols of Southern pride rather than symbols of racism. White Christians are also about 20 percentage points more likely to disagree with this statement: "Generations of slavery and discrimination have created conditions that make it difficult for Blacks to work their way out of the lower class." And these trends generally persist even in the wake of the recent protests for racial justice.[4]

What does all of this mean for me and my own deconstruction of the Evangelical mindset that I accepted for many decades? Here is the irony. It was only after I deliberately and intentionally rejected the Evangelical faith that I could finally see and understand what had been going on around me for years. That is, the structural and systematic racism that exists throughout American society. It wasn't just a personal sin anymore.

Additionally, I began to see the unconscious biases that I had that drove my decisions and actions. As an Evangelical I simply was not open to viewing myself as part of the problem. I was against racism because it was a personal sin, not a social problem or certainly not a systemic problem.

Growing up in a white protestant conservative church I rarely if ever heard a sermon about civil rights or about the sin of racism. We talked about it in our youth group meetings occasionally, and the youth leaders would all admit that racism and especially the actions of groups like the KKK were sinful. But they had accepted the Graham assumption. The only solution would come about when Christ returned or when individuals accepted Christ. In other words, it lulled us into a complacency that led to apathy about this topic. It certainly wasn't something we were ever encouraged to take action, or protest. We were encouraged to be "non-racist," but never encouraged to be "anti-racist." This is the key distinction.

Those are terms more common to recent developments and events. But the dynamics were at play even in the 1960s and 70s. Because we were all born-again Christians, we believed we were immune to charges of racism. We weren't racist. And certainly, we were not guilty of anything like slavery or Jim Crow discrimination even though our conservative church had virtually no black members. We all considered ourselves to be non-racists.

But that was the key word, "guilt." We never considered ourselves guilty of any wrongdoing in relation to blacks, Hispanics, or Native Americans because it was all a matter of personal sin not structural racism.

"Guilt" brings the issue down to what a post-Evangelical mindset has helped me to learn or relearn. After awakening from the Evangelical slumber and complacency that I was in, I was able to see that racism isn't just about personal sin or actions. But as I have engaged in various conversations with Evangelicals on this issue in the past few years the main objection I hear is about guilt. They don't in any way want to be considered guilty of the sin of racism.

If you suggest that they may have unconscious biases they think you are trying to make *them* feel guilty. If you suggest that racism is built into the core of American institutions including churches, their immediate response is, "I'm not guilty for what happened a hundred years ago, so there is no reason to discuss it now." Any discussion of racial issues is filtered through the Evangelical lens of personal sin and guilt. The Graham assumption! They consider themselves to be personally non-racist so there can be no guilt. "Besides, Jesus loves everyone and so do I."

In fact, when white Evangelicals throw up the "guilt defense" it is a tactic that goes back to Graham's theology. There is nothing we can do about racism until Jesus returns so why are you talking about it? Don't try and make me feel guilty. It is a deflection and diversionary tactic aimed at keeping Evangelicals from feeling guilt or more importantly, having to take action against racism.

What I've learned over the past several years especially since the emergence of "Black Lives Matter" and protests against police violence, is that black people aren't interested in making anyone feel guilty.

I am amazed at the reaction of Evangelicals to BLM. They are usually the first ones to counter with the worn-out disrespectful phrase, "All Lives Matter." I know because I reacted the same way. It is almost automatic. Evangelicals think when someone says, "black lives matter," it is supposed to illicit guilt. It's not. The emotion that is being called out is empathy.

So, let's delve into the difference.

Empathy, that should be a feeling and emotion that resonates with Evangelicals who claim to be followers of Christ. But empathy is rarely the reaction. It is almost axiomatic that Evangelicals will not react with empathy to the brutality and discrimination our institutions continue to heap on people of color. In fact, Evangelicals are more likely to see police brutality as the act of a few bad cops, falling back again on the personal sin narrative. They refuse to see it as part of a historic trend of law enforcement racism that has targeted people of color unfairly for decades and centuries.

As I have reached out to people of color and had conversations about this with them, never once have I ever heard someone say that they want white people to feel guilty for past actions for which they have no responsibility. But what I do hear from my black friends is that they want at least to feel empathy from white allies. They wish that white people would develop understanding of the racist system that still exists and that they might take responsibility for dismantling it now. That would require action on the part of whites.

Another word for dismantling racist systems is "anti-racist." A non-racist is only concerned about protecting their own reputations and avoiding guilt. Anti-racists recognize that racist systems that benefit white people over other groups of people still exist, and we have a responsibility to undo these systems.

Empathy is an interesting term in this context. As a young Evangelical I was able to feel badly for how Black people had been treated in the United States. But this was a detached feeling of "oh, that is a shame that slavery or discrimination happened." It was closer to pity than empathy. I could feel sorry for Black people and then move on and forget about it because I had built a wall between those actions and myself. I justified my own feeling of concern about the situation without feeling any need to correct it. After all, Jesus had forgiven me of all those sins.

Pity isn't the same as sympathy. It's important to define these terms. I couldn't feel sympathy because this word means that you have experienced or felt the same way as another person, so you understand intimately how they feel. An example is a sympathy card that you send when your friend experiences the death of someone close. You can feel sympathy because it is likely you have experienced the same sense of loss when you have lost a friend or loved one. Sympathy is an appropriate emotion to express to someone in that case. But a white person cannot have sympathy for a black person because they have never experienced the pain and suffering caused by discrimination, microaggression or other forms of marginalization.

This is why developing empathy is so important. Empathy literally means you make an effort to identify with what someone else has experienced by putting yourself in their shoes. Empathy is a function of using a powerful human tool, the imagination. Imagining what discrimination and devaluing feels like so that you understand it. Empathy and understanding go hand in hand. But empathy is hard work because you need to find a way to put yourself in their shoes. For most it is just easier to say, "sorry, I pity you, but I'm not guilty." And then move on.

There are several ways to develop empathy for the experience of people of color. The most obvious way is to simply have conversations with people of color and ask them to explain what it is like to be targeted or profiled in our society. One of the most profound conversations I've been involved with was through my work.

The non-profit company that I work for has a strong commitment to equality and diversity. We have a DEIA team in our organization which stands for "Diversity, Equity, Inclusion, and Access." One meeting the DEIA committee set up was a panel discussion with several black members of our organization who talked about their experiences. I was deeply moved by their descriptions of everyday life and how it is affected by discrimination.

One gentleman recounted that anytime he goes to a store he never leaves the store without a receipt for his purchases, and he prominently displays this receipt where all store workers can see it. He has been accused of shoplifting many times prior simply because he is black, and this is now just standard practice.

I tried to put myself in his shoes. What would that be like for me to feel compelled to display something as mundane as a receipt which I take for granted as a white person? I never think twice about a receipt and in fact many times, I even refuse to take one with me out of the store. Every time I go to a store and pick up a receipt now, I remember the pain in that man's voice. What a difference in perspective.

A friend of mine who is a black woman detailed her experience shopping in a local store recently. Our community is not very diverse, and she and her daughter are often targeted with racial slurs. But one experience stood out.

As she was shopping in the store, a white man with confederate flag patches on his jacket began to follow her in a menacing way gazing at her and making her feel unsafe. She kept moving but he kept following, and glaring. She had no idea what he might do.

Finally, this woman's husband came along who happens to be white, and the other man backed off and went away. Again, I tried to put myself in her place. How would that feel? It was something that has never happened to me. I can't experience it, but I can listen and try to understand it. As I listened to the emotion in her voice it created a sense of empathy for her. Not pity and not sympathy, but empathy.

Finally, I have made it a goal to visit historical sites around the country where various acts of racial violence and injustice have occurred. I believe that experiencing a sense of "place" is important for understanding historical events.

Recently I visited the "Whitney Plantation" in Louisiana located between New Orleans and Baton Rouge along the Mississippi River. It was at one time a major sugar plantation. It was home to thousands of enslaved people in the ante-bellum period and the plantation today specializes in a "slave tour." It is a walking tour throughout the plantation that highlights not the lives of the rich planters, but the lives of those that were ensnared and enslaved in the system. It included stories of the children that were born on the plantation into slavery, grew up there and spent their whole lives under this cruel system.

It was an emotional experience for me as I deliberately tried to put myself in their shoes as I walked through the same places they had lived and ask what it was like to be enslaved. The result of this and other exercises like it are to develop a sense of empathy. Pity is condescending and sympathy is impossible to express. But empathy is something I can develop if I work at it.

If white people would listen, ask questions, seek to understand, and put themselves in the shoes of black people, they would develop empathy, not guilt. But empathy provides the proper impulse and motive to take action.

Once I understand the plight of someone else and truly understand that as a white person, I have some power to change it, then I can become "anti-racist." Anti-racist I define as someone that has developed enough empathy for the plight of black people that they are ready to take responsibility and action.

Here is the full irony of this realization. I had to leave the church and Evangelical faith to get to this understanding and point of action. Maybe others won't have to do so, but I did. And I suspect others that are deconstructing their Evangelical faith will be able to do the same.

PART THREE

FAITH & GAY RIGHTS: LOVE IS LOVE, REGARDLESS

ELEVEN

REMEMBERING MURPH

MAY I BAKE YOUR WEDDING CAKE?

Homosexuality is a chosen behavior that is contrary to the fundamental unchanging truths that has been ordained by God in the Bible, recognized by our nation's founders, and shared by the majority of Texans.[1]

—From the **Texas Republican Party's** 2016 platform

THE HISTORY OF THE United States is one of expanding rights, generation after generation. Those opposed to constitutional rights for same sex marriage are trying to stand in the way of a giant locomotive that has been moving in one direction for over 200 years. And I find it interesting that most of the time the people who are opposed to expanded rights somehow rely on the Bible to justify their argument as if to say God is on their side. I know this too well as you will see, I was part of that culture.

Gay rights have come a long way in American culture just within my lifetime. Gays in the 1960's and 70's were still routinely objects of derision, discriminated against, made fun of, and even were objects of violence and brutality. Of course, this is still true in some quarters though hopefully it is the exception rather than the rule. Attitudes and behaviors can and do change over time and this is a hopeful and positive sign.

Now gay marriage is legal, and we had an openly gay man running for President of the United States and did quite well. Things can and do change because human beings can change.

For those that believe in American exceptionalism I would contend that America isn't exceptional because it is culturally superior to all other cultures; but there is an ability within American society to seek remedies for wrongs that it has committed and to consciously work toward social improvement. We have seen it repeatedly in the civil rights movement, women's movement, and now the gay rights movements. That is exceptional, but it is hard work and sometimes takes years to accomplish.

The past few years have been a metamorphosis for me on this issue as well. My Evangelical upbringing made tolerance for gay lifestyles out of the question and teaching in private Christian schools also meant that any hedging on this issue would raise the ire of parents, school boards, and even many students. Of course, I had doubts, but like most doubts within the Evangelical religious community you certainly didn't talk about them.

Evangelicals are still of the belief that being gay is a choice that they can choose or not choose. But the first epiphany in my little Evangelical brain was to realize that I did not at any time in my life, ever choose my own sexual orientation or preference. There was never a day where I sat down and reasoned it through and decided, "I think I'll go ahead and be attracted to the opposite sex for the rest of my life." It was just there.

I strongly suspect this is the case for those that experience same sex attraction. They have no more chosen that orientation than I did. In fact, there were many disincentives to choose that sexual orientation given the bigotry, discrimination and hostility toward gays. Why would anyone choose that fate? Who wants the abuse?

The intolerance and hostility toward gays that permeates the Evangelical community is not only distasteful but is exactly the opposite of what I read about in the New Testament in the teachings of Jesus. The love of Christ and the inclusiveness of spirituality makes the continued persecution and exclusion of gay people totally unacceptable.

Perhaps the most transformative change in my view of Christianity and the role of a Christian has been to stop defining the job of a Christian as being the behavior police going around giving out behavior citations to people that don't measure up in some way. Instead, I think my calling is to love people, period. It doesn't matter who they are, what they've done, or whether they agree with my agenda or not. I have officially turned in my behavior police badge.

As I have gone through this evolution in my thinking about Christianity in general, and how I can apply Christ's love toward gay people in particular, I have also started to remember some painful and embarrassing events from my former life as a young teenage Evangelical growing up in my safe Evangelical conservative church in Iowa.

I remember this story especially and feel compelled to share it only for my own conscience's sake and relief from the feeling of having wronged someone who didn't deserve the treatment for which I was partially responsible.

In telling this story I am not proud of the behavior and attitudes that I exhibited but I think it is still relevant to share it in light of how gays are still being treated in schools, colleges, the workplace, and yes, in churches, especially churches. For some unknown reason kids and many adults still feel they have a green light to bully and discriminate against gay people. And we see the results that many times are devastating or even deadly. It is no coincidence that young gays are four times more likely to commit suicide as their straight counterparts.[2]

My story doesn't include a suicide, at least not to my knowledge. But the disapproval that I and others heaped upon one young man in our church youth group was enough to cause hurt and damage that certainly made life for him more difficult, especially coming from the hands of those that proclaimed Christ as their personal savior.

I want to tell you about a young man named Murph. His last name was Murphy, and I honestly am not sure of his first name because most of the time we simply called him Murph. Murph was an outwardly gay individual who joined our youth group in the 1960's.

I met Murph when I was around 14 or 15 years old, in 1969. He was a year or two older than me and lived across town from where our church was located. Murph would either ride a bus to church or sometimes take a taxi to get there. He didn't have money, lived with his mother who I never saw, and his clothes were usually a bit sloppy and unkempt. I think he was from a single-parent family as I was.

We had church services on Sunday morning, a youth group meeting Sunday night, and another youth meeting or choir practice on Wednesday evening. Murph was a loyal participant in as many of these meetings as a ten-cent bus fare would allow. He seemed to love coming to our youth group which was quite sizable in number.

When we had youth meetings there were many hot topics for discussion. In the late 60's and early 70's the topics were lively. We talked about civil rights, the Vietnam War, cultural phenomenon like the hippie movement, sex, drugs and of course, rock-n-roll. But gay lifestyles never came up in these discussions as I remember because it was a taboo subject. We could talk about sex before marriage and living together vs. marriage, but gay relationships? Never on the radar.

Murph came to these meetings and shared his views and opinions like the rest of us but somehow during discussions we ended up usually dismissing his ideas. I think we didn't give Murph the credibility he deserved because well, you know, Murph was gay.

He was never included in many of our social events that were organized outside of the youth group. We were secretly and quietly embarrassed by Murph because of his effeminate manner. I'm not sure to what degree he knew that he was a second-class member of our group but as time went on, it seemed that it became more and more acceptable to exclude and even make fun of Murph for his mannerisms and orientation. And we did.

Why Murph continued to come to our youth group I'm not sure. We certainly were not showing him God's love in any meaningful way. Eventually someone tried to talk to him to literally, straighten him out. But Murph simply dismissed their reprimands and continued to come to the group and continued to be gay.

I suspect that Murph was also trying to figure out his own life as we all were at that age. He wanted the friendship and fellowship that our group provided but it became harder and harder for him to be himself as we became more "committed Christians." What an oxymoron.

Here is the kicker, as we were "growing in our faith" we were becoming more and more intolerant and less loving toward someone like Murph. This makes no sense to me at all now but for some reason, the Evangelical mindset gave us permission to treat Murph in anything but a loving way.

Although the behavior was my decision and mine alone, the Evangelical environment encouraged such condescension and arrogance. How this saddens me today to think of how unloving we were, I was.... toward another human being in the name of false righteousness. We were playing behavior police, proudly handing out behavior citations for God, with clobber Bible verses written all over them.

The final straw for Murph came at a youth retreat that our group held one year. This was the usual spiritual retreat designed to get everyone to fall under the conviction of the Holy Spirit mainly through guilt and shame, so that everyone realized what awful people they were so they would fling themselves yet once again on the mercy of God. The whole retreat is manipulated toward this rising emotional crescendo and there is at the climax of the event, an altar call, where kids would go forward to weep and wallow in self-absorption and repentance.

This particular retreat also had a fun side to it. There was a talent show one night which was a bit of an open mic, silly sketch event where everyone did something absurd. The more absurd the better and everyone laughed and had a good time.

When Murph's moment came, he walked out on the platform in drag doing an imitation of Mae West and as I remember, a very good one at that. For anyone younger than 40 or so, you may want to google Mae West. She was the movie star diva of the 1920's and 30's and her persona included a raw sexuality that was quite scandalous for her time. Murph's depiction of her was over the top but funny in hindsight.

Unfortunately, several leaders in the youth group didn't see the humor so much and decided that they needed to confront Murph about his obvious gay proclivities. Being part of the leadership by that time I was part of the Bible lynch mob that cornered Murph that night. There were 3 or 4 of us that were pounding him with the clobber verses from the Bible about what a horrible sin being gay was. Although I don't think this was motivated by hate or was meant to be harassment the result was the same. I don't think anyone stopped long enough to consider his feelings or the impact of our hurtful words.

The assumption on our part was that Murph had simply chosen this orientation and that he could just as easily UN-choose it somehow. I can only imagine the loneliness and alienation that Murph must have felt that night. We all felt so smugly self-righteous and arrogantly spiritual about it.

Murph slept that night alone, no one wanted to sleep near him in the bunk area because he slept in his Mae West costume. I believe Murph was hurt to the core and devastated by our attempt to "speak the truth in love." It was anything but loving and it wasn't even the truth.

It wasn't long after that retreat that Murph stopped coming to our youth group meetings. He may have come once or twice more but then he dropped off the map completely. I know he didn't feel welcome any longer if he ever did. And instead of showing any concern to reach out to him we felt relieved we didn't have to deal with the "Murph problem" anymore.

Murph did contact us several months later and invited some of us to come to his new church home one Friday night. They had their own coffee house on Friday nights, and he wanted to show it off. A couple of us went over there and shock of shocks we had walked into a gay coffee house.

Apparently, this church openly accepted gays and provided a safe place for them to socialize. I remember the sense of uneasiness and a disconcerting feeling of being in the minority for once. It was a shock to my Evangelical pea brain that there were people that called themselves Christian but were actively and openly gay.

Of course, we felt we had to fix these people, so we got into a heated theological debate with some of the leaders of the coffee house. Out came the clobber verses. Then I heard for the first time an actual reasonable refutation of these said verses. At the time I thought these folks were just deluded and they were distorting the word of God, but it was a startling conversation.

I found out that there were indeed other ways to look at these verses beside the one I was taught. I think that conversation planted a seed of doubt within me that over the course of several decades would come to full bloom. I'm a slow learner.

We left the coffee house after the discussion, and I never saw Murph again. I don't know what became of him, but it seemed that he had found a home. I sincerely hope that he found the love, acceptance, and the support that we did not provide him.

Looking back on this experience I know and understand now that this was a classic case of putting dogma before people and the worship of literal Biblicism ahead of loving others. I've come to see myself and the other youth leaders in the role of Pharisees who Jesus roundly condemns over and over in the New Testament for doing exactly the same thing. We put religious stumbling blocks in front of people who are simply looking for God's love somewhere and not finding it in a church, at least not ours.

I can only say that looking at it today, I wish there were do-overs. But the one thing I can do now is advocate and work toward a more enlightened sense of what the teachings of Jesus are on this subject, and just about every other subject on which I have had to unlearn the literal biblical dogma. Literalism kills life. It is a distortion because it causes Christians to put ideology and even their precious morality ahead of people.

So Murph if you are out there, I do hope that you have found the love of your life. I hope that you have found acceptance and support from Christians that are far more enlightened than me and my group. I can only ask that you forgive me for my ignorance and misplaced priorities; for making you to feel like a second-class human being and somehow less deserving of God's love than straight people. And if you decide to get married to your partner, I would be willing to buy your cake for you, or better yet, let me bake you one.

TWELVE

SPREAD MORE LOVE THAN HATE (LIKE CARLA)

BY MEREDITH HENDERSON

The story below was written as a Facebook post by my wonderful daughter, Meredith Henderson, the day that the Supreme Court ruled in favor of recognizing same-sex marriage. That day was a day to celebrate love and to show the world that love wins and will always conquer hate. The reaction of the members of the AME Church in Charleston in the aftermath of that horrible shooting have also bore witness to the power of love. Dr. Martin Luther King Jr. once said, "I have decided to stick with love . . . Hate is too great a burden to bear." This story will show just how right Dr. King was. Saying "love wins" is not a cliché, but a powerful life force from which anyone that is confronted with hatred can draw strength and ability to choose a different way. Jesus once said, "Love those that hate you and pray for those that persecute you." These are powerful realities if people will have the courage to follow them. I hope you will be moved by this story, as I was. Enjoy.

We are moving into our new home tomorrow, and I should be packing. And I was packing, but I had to stop and take a break in light of the amazing news that today has gifted. So, this is going to be one of those long and sappy statuses (FB), and I won't know if you just keep scrolling, so no offense taken, if you do smiley emoticons.

I remember a time not long ago when I wasn't too confident that our country would legalize same-sex marriage in any states, but to grant this right in all 50 states didn't even seem like a remote possibility. Yet, here we are. I've been able to stop blubbering long enough to remember something that I experienced in 2005, during Pride in Des Moines. A few friends and I were at the Pride picnic, the day before the parade. It was a time for members and allies of the LGBT community and their families to come share a meal, make friends, and socialize. However, it was a big park. There were other people there that day, and apparently those people didn't seem to like that we were having a picnic in the same area.

The name calling, most of us ignored. We rolled our eyes, as most people there were, sadly, used to this kind of thing. Some teenage girls came over to the picnic area, name calling, yelling, and being generally terrible towards a group of strangers who were just trying to enjoy a sunny day amongst friends. Again, they were ignored. Yes, we heard it, but no one was going to acknowledge such mean spirited, immature behavior. They must have realized they were being ignored, because soon, the rude comments turned into throwing rocks. First one, then handfuls. Several people were hit with them. We couldn't very well ignore them anymore. A couple of people threatened to call authorities. This didn't seem to faze these girls. They continued to throw rocks, calling out derogatory names towards complete strangers, all while their parents watched from afar, and did nothing.

Then there was Carla. A woman who had been enjoying the picnic with her family and friends. She did not threaten to call the police. Carla, based on her physical stature, seemed like the sort of person like getting on her bad side would be a terrible idea. Yet, she walked up to the girls with a smile. We all watched Carla in awe. Was she crazy? She asked the girls why they were doing this. The girls didn't really have much to say. Carla continued to, in the most loving way imaginable, ask why they would want to treat people this way when we had done nothing to them. The girls were quiet, finally.

Then Carla said something I have never forgotten. "I know you think we're different. But we're just like you. And we just want everyone to know we're not bad people. We want you to understand we're just people." The girls looked like they just saw a ghost. They finally realized how they had acted was unacceptable.

We thought that's how it would end. Carla had other plans. She asked the girls to come over to our picnic and first, apologize, and secondly, grab a plate of food and talk to a few people. To ask questions, if they wanted. My jaw dropped. But they did.

The girls came over, and they apologized. Carla took them to the food area and helped them get a plate of food. Then she invited them out for conversation with her family and friends. At one point, the girls ended up next to me. I was with a couple of friends, one of who was beginning transition as a transgendered woman and was wearing women's clothing. The girls stared at her, unsure what to think. My friend smiled back. Then one of the girls said "I like your pants. They're cute." And from there, they had a long, lovely, girly conversation about fashion. I was shocked. I looked at Carla. She must have seen the shock on my face. She just smiled and walked away. The girls continued to socialize with people, and eventually went on their way.

The next day, I marched in the Pride parade. On the route, I looked to my left, and saw Carla and her family sitting on the curb. I waved. She waved and smiled back. I never knew her last name, I didn't get any contact information, although I wish I had. She taught me one of the biggest lessons I've ever learned. You cannot fight a cause of love with hate. Love always wins. So, here's to you, Carla, wherever you are. Here's to all the LGBT community. Here's to our country. And, as always, here's to love.

THIRTEEN

CUSTER'S LAST STAND

THE IRRELEVANCE OF EVANGELICAL CHRISTIANITY IN THE 21ST CENTURY

"Destiny guides our fortunes more favorably than we could have expected. Look there, Sancho Panza, my friend, and see those thirty or so wild giants, with whom I intend to do battle and kill each and all of them, so with their stolen booty we can begin to enrich ourselves. This is nobel, righteous warfare, for it is wonderfully useful to God to have such an evil race wiped from the face of the earth."

"What giants?" Asked Sancho Panza.

"The ones you can see over there," answered his master, "with the huge arms, some of which are very nearly two leagues long."

"Now look, your grace," said Sancho, "what you see over there aren't giants, but windmills, and what seems to be arms are just

their sails, that go around in the wind and turn the millstone."

"Obviously," replied Don Quixote, "you don't know much about adventures."

—**Miguel de Cervantes**, *Don Quixote*

On June 25, 1876, General George Custer rode out for the last time along the banks of the Little Bighorn River and attacked a group of Lakota and Cheyenne Indians. Due to his arrogance, hubris, sense of entitlement and belief in his own infallibility, he led 265 men to their deaths. Every one of them was wiped out. It was needless, pointless, and perhaps the worst defeat of the US Calvary in the Indian Wars on the Plains in the 19th Century.

I thought of this historical event while thinking about the state of Oregon's decision in handing down a $135,000 fine to the owners of *Sweet Cakes Bakery* for refusing to provide a wedding cake for a lesbian couple in 2013.

"Christians, get ready to take a stand," Aaron Klein, one of the bakery's co-owners, told *The Blaze*. "Get ready for civil disobedience."

Really? Over a cake? The Evangelical community lit up with cries of religious discrimination and loss of religious freedom because they were forced to bake a cake for a gay couple. Christians seemed ready to make a last stand on the hillside of gay marriage.

It reminds me of Custer riding gallantly to his own death, assured of the rightness of his cause and motivated by a manifest destiny that gave him and others a sense that slaughtering Native Americans was something which God would approve. Baking a cake for a gay couple may just be the Evangelical church's last stand in the 21st Century.

In the first decade of the 21st Century Evangelicals made up approximately 30% of the U.S. population. However, since 2007, this percentage has declined to around 23%, and even more among young people. One of the main reasons young people are leaving is the antiquated view on social issues, including gay rights.

I count myself among this group even though I'm no longer "young." Could it be that people are finding the church so irrelevant not only on a personal level, but on a societal level, that they are beginning to leave the church in droves? The point is that American culture is finding Christianity increasingly irrelevant and unimportant in their lives. I can't help but think that refusing to bake a cake, as symbolic of the last stand of Christian faith in America, will only hasten the decline and marginalization of the church.

Evangelicals seem to think that others are doing this to them, that they are the victims of some liberal conspiracy or bias when in reality they are riding to their own demise just like Custer, for a literalist and inerrant interpretation of a few bible passages.

I think the hubris goes further. Evangelicals are making this last stand because they see their privileged status as the religion of choice in American society slipping farther and farther away. And rather than engaging in any critical self-examination to determine just why the church is becoming increasingly irrelevant, they are wallowing in self-pity and claiming martyrdom at the hands of liberals, progressives, secularists, and other "godless" types. It seems that wedding cakes could well be the Little Bighorn of Evangelicalism.

It used to be that churches were engaged in meaningful and significant causes throughout American history.

In my own study of American history and as a teacher of history, I took great interest and enthusiasm in looking for the positive involvement of American churches in many important reform movements. From the earliest days of the American Republic, Christians were often motivated to seek reforms and to right the wrongs of society and improve the lives of the neglected and marginalized. Here are just a few examples:

British reformer and member of Parliament, William Wilberforce was a thundering voice against slavery and the slave trade and helped to bring this institution to an end in England in 1807. He inspired the US abolitionist movement.

Even though slave owners of the south used the Bible to justify slavery and even cruelty, many, if not most of the abolitionists of the 19th Century, were motivated by Christian morality.

The Quakers stand out as the earliest Christians calling for abolition. The beginnings of the Quakers' opposition came in 1657, when their founder, George Fox, wrote "To Friends beyond sea, that have Blacks and Indian slaves" to remind them of the Quaker belief in equality. For them, abolition was as much about spreading Christian ethics as it was ending slavery, and the two went hand-in-hand.

In America in the 19th Century, the evangelical preacher, Wendell Phillips, was perhaps one of the most effective leaders in the fight for abolition of slavery, women's rights, and equal rights for Native Americans in the pre-Civil War era.

John Wesley was an early leader in the Methodist movement. Under his direction, Methodists became leaders in many areas of social justice, including prison reform and the abolition of the Slave Trade.

Other Christian reformers of the 19th Century fought for more humane treatment for the insane; better treatment for criminals and improvement of the prison system; protection for children in the burgeoning factory system; and protection and rights for women who were still powerless in American society.

Catholic social justice leaders such as Father John Ryan and Dorothy Day pushed for similar values and engaged in religious activism. In the 20th Century, Walter Rauschenbusch published his Social Gospel classic *Christianity and the Social Crisis* in 1907 and this had a profound impact on Protestants of all denominations.

Many Christians worked for the improvement of sanitation in American cities, for the rights of workers, established settlement houses, the rights of migrant workers, for the protection of the environment, and other worthy causes.

Finally, the Civil Rights movement was largely motivated by the preaching of Evangelical pastors and leaders such as the Rev. Martin Luther King, and countless other pastors and preachers. The moral persuasion of the non-violence movement, bolstered by the Christian message, brought massive changes for the better to American society.

These were causes for which the Christian message resonated and were worthy of the teachings of Jesus. The teachings of Christ that focused on standing with the weak, the neglected, the marginalized and the powerless found expression in Christian activists of these earlier times. And it is no coincidence that church attendance in these earlier eras were much higher than today. Church affiliation and attendance had purpose, calling, a focus on justice and a vision of a righteous and caring society.

Today, the Christian message is equated with refusing to bake a cake. Yes, it's about a cake!

Christians want to make their final stand on this issue; the right to discriminate against a group of people because in their eyes, they are sinners of the worst kind. How ridiculously self-righteous, self-absorbed, and arrogant this sounds to a society that has moved beyond such a petty view.

To be sure, there are causes and issues for which the Christian message can resonate today. In fact, one could say that our society needs a Christian influence, voice, and presence for many of these issues if no other reason than a large portion of people still identify with that religion. The Christians that still make up the religious majority could have a significant impact on our culture if harnessed toward worthy causes. Here are some examples of issues we are facing that the church could play a vital positive role to provide leadership and a spiritual dynamic for action:

Sex trafficking: Sex traffickers use violence, threats, lies, debt bondage, and other forms of coercion to force women and children to engage in commercial sex against their will. In 2019, the *National Human Trafficking*

Resource Center hotline received reports of 4,460 sex trafficking cases inside the United States.[1] This practice is tantamount to modern day slavery, and yet, Evangelicals are worried about baking a cake for a gay couple.

Racial Terrorism: Black churches are under attack particularly in the south, through shootings, church burnings, campaigns of fear and intimidation and the presences of dozens of hate groups of which many claim Christian motivations. These are brothers and sisters in Christ and fellow human beings that are experiencing true terrorism on a daily basis and yet, Evangelicals are worried about baking a cake for the wrong people.

A Culture of Violence: The U.S. has the highest violence and gun death ratios of any industrialized nation on earth.[2] Children are most often the victim of this violence whether it is from a domestic source, a school shooting, a neighborhood drug thug, or even suicide. Many of these deaths are accidental, but many can be prevented. And yet, Evangelicals seem more worried about baking a cake against their will.

Growing Poverty Rates: 37.2 million Americans are still stuck under the poverty line, even in the wake of a recovering economy.[3] Once again, children are the main victims of growing poverty and the "free-reduced" lunch rates in schools have generally more than doubled since 2007. (U.S. Census Report, 2020) In the nation's richest country, we cannot even find a way to support working families that are in poverty, and yet, Evangelicals are concerned about their so-called freedom to not bake a cake for gay couples.

Highest Incarceration Rates in the Developed World. The U.S. rate is 358 prisoners per 100,000 residents or about 1.3 million prisoners in 2020, according to the latest available data from the *Bureau of Justice Statistics* (BJS).[4] By comparison, the rate in other comparable countries is around 100 per 100,000. Incarceration falls inequitably on the young, blacks, Latinos, the poor, and less educated. The church could make an impact on this phenomenon if focus, resources, and priorities were changed; but instead, Evangelicals wring their hands about baking a cake.

Political Corruption of our Political System: Corporations have purchased, and some say hijacked the political system which now works primarily in their favor to curry lower taxes, impact legislation to favor their investments, and work against the needs of the middle and lower classes. Unlike gay marriage, Jesus was unequivocal about the economic exploitation that the wealthy class in his day heaped upon the marginalized and the poor. The church can change this system if it stops worrying about who they will be baking a cake for.

Evangelicals need to get over themselves and realize that they are not being persecuted, they are not losing their religious liberty so long as you don't define liberty as the freedom to discriminate against a class of people. They are still the preferred religion of our culture, and no one is being jailed, persecuted, or denied the right to gather in a house of worship.

For too long the church has used its preferred status to squander opportunity after opportunity to lead a charge against some of the worst problems our society has faced over the past 30 or 40 years, to focus on insignificant issues, petty issues, or sideshow issues. This is in large part due to the entanglement of Evangelical churches with Republican Party politics which has co-opted the message of Christ and turned it into a witch hunt for all things non-conservative and anti-Republican, and to win votes above all other priorities.

If church affiliation and attendance, especially by younger Americans, is dwindling, don't blame the liberal media, don't blame godless humanists, and don't blame the devil. Blame yourselves, look in the mirror and ask some tough questions. This trend will continue until American Christianity shrinks into the oblivion of its last stand.

It is NOT about a cake, it is about survival as a vibrant-relevant institution that needs to reflect the love of God for all people, provide aid and help for those that are marginalized in a power-hungry society, and lead a charge against some of the worst ills of our age. We need a vibrant spiritual community to rise up to meet these challenges, but not to make a last stand on top of a gay wedding cake.

FOURTEEN

WHAT STRAIGHT MEN NEED TO LEARN FROM GAY MEN, ABOUT LOVING WOMEN

Finally, straight women love gay men because they are emotionally attracted to the fearlessness and lack of self-consciousness in gay men. In general, gay men, and gay women, too, tend to be more fearless than their straight counterparts—particularly straight men—because they've usually experienced bullying and prejudice because of their sexual orientation. These experiences fortify gay men with thicker skin. As out adults, gay men usually learn to accept themselves and stop trying so hard to win the approval and acceptance of others.[1]

—**Seth Meyers**, Clinical Psychologist

I READ AN ARTICLE from *Psychology Today*, called, "Why Straight Women Are Attracted to Gay Men," published by Seth Meyers Psy.D., Jul 06, 2012.[2] This article intrigued me for several reasons especially in the current context of the "Me-too" movement and the public statements of sexual conquest bragged about by a former President.

Had I read this article from a prior lens of Evangelical Christianity, I would have dismissed it as liberal-humanistic trash to be ignored or even burned. In Evangelical faith, anything that threatens to change or challenge the gender power relationship is to be condemned. And, because the article doesn't judge homosexuality or call it a sin, the article would be considered an endorsement of "sin." Patriarchy is considered "God's plan for families." A straight female-gay male relationship has no place in that theology.

Growing up in an Evangelical church, messages of patriarchy were everywhere, from the lack of any female leadership within the church, to sermons preached about the leadership role of men, women's subordinate role, and "God's order" for the family and society. Women were always in the back seat, silenced, and devalued.

These images and messages of patriarchy were particularly confusing to a young male being raised in a single-parent home by his mother. What were you to make of female leadership at home when the message was clear that men should be in charge?

It also interfered with learning how to develop relationships with the opposite sex as a teenager and a young man coming of age at a time with the women's liberation movement emerged and challenged these archaic ideas. It brought so many questions to mind:

What is the proper Biblical view of manhood? Womanhood? Equality? Roles?

How do you learn to love and respect someone who is your "lesser" in God's order?

What I can tell you first-hand is that it created a toxic brew of arrogance, pride, and misogyny. All of it justified with Bible verses and sermon tapes.

After leaving Evangelical Christianity behind and coming to a new understanding about love and accepting gay relationships as another expression of that love, I started to notice things I hadn't before.

I began to see that some females had marvelous and fulfilling friendships with gay men. This was something I would never have considered as acceptable as an Evangelical. It wasn't just one, it was everywhere I looked or listened that women were expressing their admiration and love for a gay male friend and sought out their friendship.

I saw this type of relationship from a personal acquaintance. I have a former colleague from work who is still a friend of mine, that has an interesting relationship with a male gay friend. In sharing her story, I will change the names and context to protect their privacy.

Sheila and Robert have been friends for over 10 years. They met working in the same company and even after both moved on from that company, they have remained close personal friends. Robert is a gay man who is married to his partner, and Sheila is straight and married. Sometimes the four of them go out together, and sometimes just Sheila and Robert go out.

They have a friendship that Sheila describes as "a level playing field." Because Robert is gay there are no worries or expectations about a sexual relationship so she reports that she can feel comfortable and safe. They meet frequently and Robert will go shopping with her occasionally which she says she hates to do, but Robert has a great eye for fashion. While shopping she reports that other women have said they wished they had a gay friend like Robert to help them pick out clothes.

The "level playing field" is a critical part of this relationship. Sheila says, "one of the things I appreciate about my relationship with Robert is - I can share ideas and opinions with a man, and he listens to them and values them. In the work climate, at least in mine right now, it is all run by men and women's opinions often get brushed aside. We often joke that they'd listen to us if we at least held up a fake mustache." This was a key component of their relationship that Sheila says makes it so important to her.

What I found intriguing in Robert and Sheila's relationship was that she valued his male companionship because he still brought a male perspective to topics and issues. Yet, he accepted her as an equal, had no expectations, and valued her opinions as much as anyone else.

Perhaps another way to say it is, Sheila's relationship with Robert is not based on patriarchy. It is the rare time when a straight man and woman can have a co-equal relationship where power doesn't play a nuanced or overt role. With Robert she is free to be herself because there is no patriarchal rule to govern their relationship.

Then I read Seth Meyer's article from 2012 and realized there was a whole area of solid research behind these observations. I believe that straight men in the United States can learn a great deal about the proper way to relate to, care for, and love the women in their lives by examining how gay men relate to women.

Starting with my prior Evangelical brain which inculcated a male-dominated view of society and relations with women, I have had to unlearn many of the nuances of male-female relationships that are the residue of that patriarchal thinking.

To begin, giving up any male-image of "God" was a good starting point. I know, I know, the Bible refers to God in the male gender as a "Father." But this view was the product of ancient Iron-Age civilizations and the product of Greco-Roman culture, which were also extremely male-dominated. This male-dominated culture certainly seeped into early Christian culture and writings, and consequently into the conservative religious thinking today. But I see no mandate today in the 21st Century, to think of God in any gender terms at all, but certainly not as a male figure.

In many circles of Evangelical Christianity and especially in some of the more fundamentalist lines the male-dominated perspective is not even nuanced, it is taught as a scriptural mandate and obligation. Thus, we end up with groups like the "Quiver-full" movement where sexual indiscretions by males are considered youthful experimentation and a "mistake" and not a violation of civil law. Or worse, these indiscretions are framed as the girl's fault for the way they dressed or appeared. It is patriarchy 101.

There are some fundamentalist preachers that teach that for a woman to refuse sex for her husband is a sin...in other words, marital rape is commanded by God. Women must submit to it. And sexual indiscretions by youth pastors and senior pastors in the Southern Baptist church are struggling to come to terms with their home-made problem. The solution is to cover it up, and let the patriarchy continue.

Even in more moderate Evangelical groups, teachings on male-dominated family structure and relationships are still the norm. The degree to which the United States is a "Judeo-Christian" culture, those elements of patriarchy are still in many ways the norm and are common and expected in male-female relationships.

But this male superiority consciousness has consequences. Abuse and rape.

According to the "Rape, Abuse and Incest National Network" (RAINN) one out of every six women has been the victim of an attempted or completed rape in her lifetime.[3] Put in other terms that is about 17.6% of women will have been raped or victim of attempted rape, which translates to about 17.7 million women.

There has been some progress in the area of sexual harassment. Sexual harassment is similar to civil rights for blacks in that it is no longer acceptable to engage in sexual harassment or other forms of power-dominated sexual control in the workplace. Laws are in place to protect women from such abuse.

Just as laws are in place to protect Black people from racial discrimination and segregation the residue of racism still exists in hearts and minds. And, for women the problem of rape, sexual abuse, and domestic violence is still an ever-present danger. Patriarchy is alive and well in the 21st Century.

Of course, none of this is new. Rape and sexual exploitation have been happening since the beginning. And earlier eras were certainly worse, and in fact, in many cultures in the world today, the treatment of women is no better than that of chattel.

I challenge men in the U.S. Even though we have come a long way, are we really at a point where we can stop evolving, changing and improving as a species as it relates to male-female relationships? The statistics I've already quoted tell us that we still have a long way to go.

That brings me back to the article and the advent of the acceptance of gay marriage and the gay orientation in general in American society. I am hopeful that this new development and acceptance will inject a new way for men to begin to adjust their view of women and how they relate to them.

If you were to ask any woman what it is they find appealing about having a male gay friend, there would be similar responses that would include:

1. **Feeling safe**
2. **Feeling respected**
3. **Feeling equal**
4. **Feeling accepted**
5. **Being able to let down self-protective boundaries and enjoy real friendship**

All these feelings should be and need to be byproducts of healthy heterosexual male-female relationships. But how many women can honestly say they feel these things in the presence of a new dating partner, boyfriend or even their husband?

To be sure, many women are fortunate enough to be able to say yes to this, but as the statistics show, large numbers of women cannot share this wonderful experience. Their experience with men in their lives is unfortunately one of abuse, despair, fear, and a sense of feeling worthless.

I suspect this is the reason women feel so much affinity and love for gay men. Typically, when a woman meets a man for the first time, they are on guard against the power dynamic of exploitation. But research shows that once a woman discovers a new male acquaintance is gay a friendship evolves much more quickly and to deeper levels.

Women report feeling respected and accepted for who they are just as Sheila relates. Gay men seem to be able to respect women as equals and accept them for who they are and not what a Hollywood image of a woman should be.

How often do straight men make comments about the models they see on television, or even other women walking down the street...in the presence of their significant other? These comments and "looks" are so disrespectful to the personhood of their wife because it objectifies women as sexual objects.

Going deeper, according to the Meyer's article,

> Straight women love gay men because closeness with gay men provides a window into how the minds of men work, something that women want to know as they navigate dating waters with their straight male peers.[4]

Gay men are still men, and though they are oriented differently in many respects, they still share many of the same thought processes, insecurities, and characteristics as straight men. A relationship with a gay man is like a relationship laboratory for a woman to learn in a safe zone, how a man thinks because the gay man typically isn't trying to hide anything to impress a woman. Most straight men are afraid to let down the boundaries of their pretend macho-male TV hero image to let a woman know how they truly think or more importantly, feel.

Perhaps one of the more interesting and not so obvious benefits of a woman's relationship with a gay man is this observation from Meyers:

> Straight women love gay men because they are emotionally attracted to the fearlessness and lack of self-consciousness in gay men. In general, gay men—and gay women, too—tend to be more fearless than their straight counterparts—particularly straight men—because they've usually experienced bullying and prejudice because of their sexual orientation, and these experiences fortify gay men with thicker skin.[5]

Interesting, gay men are actually, well, tougher than straight men emotionally. How non-stereotypical is that? Straight men put on so many masks and false images to cover up any perceived lack of strength or "manliness." It is as if the "patriarchy" requires certain qualities of a man that produces insecurities because these qualities are unreachable and are unrealistic.

As a straight man myself there is a constant internal battle to develop self-awareness about the patriarchal attitudes and impulses that have been part of my consciousness for the past 60 years. These are not easy to change.

But perhaps by seeing how gay men relate to women and provide emotional safety, respect, a sense of equality and fearlessness when it comes to sharing heart to heart on an emotional level, even an old dog like me is able to develop some new ways of relating to the opposite sex.

Here is the bottom line that I think is true. Gay men are expressing a feminine side that exists in all men. These characteristics that make women feel safe and secure are not exclusive to gay men. All men have this ability if they will develop an inner connection to it and overcome the unconscious pull of patriarchy.

By looking at the role models of how gay men express these inner qualities, and being open to them I think can help straight men to find a new way to express their masculinity without the patriarchal BS.

It doesn't mean that you will become gay or less manly, but it will challenge your basic assumptions about what those characteristics of manliness are and what they mean. And it will be necessary to shed the more archaic "Biblical teachings" that have infected the evangelical brain over the years; myself included.

PART FOUR

HOW EVANGELICAL IDEOLOGY THREATENS THE CULTURE

FIFTEEN

HOW THE RELIGIOUS RIGHT THREATENS CHRISTIANITY AND THE NATION

Onward, Christian soldiers, marching as to war,
With the cross of Jesus going on before!
Christ, the royal Master, leads against the foe;
Forward into battle, see his banner go!
Onward, Christian soldiers, marching as to war,
With the cross of Jesus going on before!

—S. Baring-Gould

WHEN I ATTENDED SUNDAY School we always sang "Onward Christian Soldiers' right next to "God Bless America." It was a good, ole' time religion and it inculcated within me a sense that to be an American meant that you were also a Christian, but not just any Christian. You had to be a patriotic Christian or more accurately, a nationalistic Christian. Thus, American culture was awash with Christian themes, symbols, messages, and other images of this unholy alliance between nationalism and Evangelicalism for decades.

In Sunday school we would say the Pledge of Allegiance and in the next breath say the "Christian Pledge of Allegiance."

"I pledge allegiance to the Christian Flag and to the Savior for whose kingdom it stands: one brotherhood, uniting all mankind, in service and love."

The message was hard to miss. Both flags stood side by side. To be a good citizen, one had to be a good Christian, and to be a good Christian, one had to be a good citizen.

Here is the nuance, being an Evangelical in the pre-1980's meant supporting the government and seeing the United States as something good and positive. This was an Americanized version of Christianity and I suspect it is what many Evangelicals were referring to when they wistfully hoped to make America great again with the election of Donald Trump in 2016.

As I studied the bible and the life and teachings of Jesus, I now realize that the Christianity I was indoctrinated into during my formative years, was a dumbed down version of the real thing, authentic Christianity. The teachings of the first Century Jewish mystic and rabbi, Jesus, are lost in the clutter of the Americanized version of Nationalistic Christianity.

Becoming a teenager in the 1960's and subsequently a Jesus freak, it was hard to reconcile this idea of Christian nationalism in the midst of the Vietnam War, the Civil Rights movement and other cultural changes that were taking place. We protested the war and stood for Civil Rights. After all, Christians should stand for peace and equal rights?

I quickly found out that this wasn't so. The major retort that I heard from good nationalistic Christians was "*America – love it or leave it.*" Christian Nationalism forbade questioning or opposing anything our righteous leaders, like Richard Nixon, were doing.

The Nixon White House was the nerve center of an attempt to create a nation-wide revival for the purpose, I can only imagine, of improving the President's approval ratings and support for his policies in an attempt to counter the anti-war protesters that were frequenting the capital in those years. The "silent majority" was the Christian majority and Billy Graham himself was the ever-present White House proof that God had his hand on the Republican administration.

In the 1960's and early 70's, Evangelicals were supporters of the government not opposed to it. Evidence Nixon's major landslide victory in 1972 thanks in large part to Evangelical Christians especially in the south. To be a good Christian, you had to support our leaders and not question what they did. Government was viewed as the righteous arm of a Christian nation that propagated only virtuous policy.

How did a giant reversal happen so that today, most Evangelicals characterize the government as the right hand of Satan? Today, Evangelicals view the government as the enemy, not a partner, especially when in the control of a Democratic president. Many even condone violence to overthrow an "evil" government.

In the 1970's I began to sense a change in the identity of the Evangelical movement. Christianity was becoming increasingly politicized. In 1976, a truly avowed Evangelical, Jimmy Carter, became President of the United States. His Baptist and born-again credentials made him the darling of the Evangelical movement, briefly. I remember hearing preachers say things such as, "he says he loves Jesus, and that's good enough for me."

Carter was a Democrat and was in favor of a woman's right to choose an abortion in the wake of *Roe v. Wade.* He also oversaw the worst economy in the post-war period and seemed to be weak in foreign policy. By 1980, a major shift would take place. The Evangelical Nationalist bus bypassed the Democrats and stopped at the door of the Republican National Convention.

Others have written about the emergence of the religious right and its historical roots. I will simply call it the "Great Convergence." By that I mean, by 1980, several forces were converging to make evangelicals a potent political force combined with an anti-government rhetoric and belief system.

The candidacy of Ronald Reagan converged with the pro-life movement, the anti-segregation movement and merged with the modern conservative political machine. This turned Evangelicals almost overnight, into Republicans. Evangelicals have voted Republican overwhelmingly in every Presidential contest since, and in hundreds of local elections.

One of the chief results of this convergence was a more anti-government stance that grew out of Reagan's political philosophy and a so-called evil government that approved abortion, and the ended Bible reading and prayer in public schools, which had taken place in the 1960's. Oh, and a government that forced integration of schools and other public places.

Religious conservatives now saw the government as the chief evil incarnate in American society, and the only solution was for Evangelicals to take over all levels of government from local school boards, to city and state government, and to national levels of office. Jerry Falwell's "Moral Majority" led the bandwagon to electoral victory after electoral victory.

Although I took part in some of this Christian nationalism in the 1980's such as anti-abortion rallies, prayer breakfasts, and other "godly" political events, I couldn't help but feel very uneasy about some of the things I heard coming out of the mouths of fellow Christians and even my own mouth. I heard some say that AIDS and gays are the reason God is judging this country. Abortion will lead us to the destruction of our civilization, and there were even those that justified using violent tactics to save innocent lives by taking an abortion doctor's life. And in some quarters, I still heard racist sentiment from the mouths of the faithful.

The other element of the right-wing Christian nationalism that was emerging in the 80's was the idea that there could be no compromise politically. These folks were playing a zero-sum game of all or nothing politics. Never mind that the whole democratic process and the Constitution was built on the concept of consensus building and compromise. Christian nationalists saw political contests in apocalyptic terms. One could not compromise with evil liberal secularists. They are godless and are the root cause of the nation's problems. They are likely socialists and communists. Only when these sinners are eradicated, and good Christian folk are in power will the nation be able to return to normalcy which was defined as a Christian nation under God.

This concept gained theological support from a "quiet" movement in the 1980's called the "Dominionists" or "Reconstructionists." These Evangelicals taught that it was God's mandate that Christians should rule all institutions of society from education to government and even to the entertainment industry. Many of them have been quietly working toward these goals ever since. Simply look into the background of several of the Republican candidates that ran in 2016 and look for the connections to Dominionist theology. These folks are dangerously close to advocating for an American Christian-Theocracy; the crown jewel of Christian Nationalism.

The two leading advocates of this so-called theology are Gary North and David Barton.

Gary North, an economic-historian, said,

> We must use the doctrine of religious liberty to gain independence for Christian schools until we train up a generation of people who know that there is no religious neutrality, no neutral law, no neutral education, and no neutral civil government. Then they will get busy in constructing a Bible-based social, political and religious order which finally denies the religious liberty of the enemies of God.[1]

David Barton, a self-styled historian, founded "Wall Builders" under the belief that the founding fathers were all Christians that wanted the United States to be governed according to Christian principles. He helped to create the narrative that the "Wall of Separation" between church and state was only to prevent a single denomination from running the government, but not to prevent Christians and Christian principles to be the basis for government. He has become the darling of the Tea Party since 2010. Barton says, "That wall is a one directional wall. It keeps the government from running the church, but it makes sure that Christian principles will always stay in government."[2]

These fellows are serious, and they have the ear of the Republican Party and funding from powerful conservative benefactors. And Republican Party operatives and power brokers are happy to use this religious element and impulse to further their grip on political power. Whether they will enact any policy to satisfy the Christian Nationalists or not is yet to be seen, but their track record on this point is dismal.

Here is the main point I want to make about Nationalistic Christianity: the use of religious faith in the pursuit of political power, social engineering, or establishment of a Christian theocracy has only one winner; the politicians and corporations, in other words, the already powerful. This goal only damages the true spiritual nature of Christianity. And, both sides can fall into this trap, conservatives, and progressives. Any attempt to politicize the faith right or left, diminishes faith and spirituality.

I recoil now when well-meaning people use the Bible and their theology to support a candidate, condemn a political opponent, or otherwise seek to enhance the political standing and power of their group, be it the religious right, or the religious left. I am certain this is not the meaning of the gospel, the *good* news.

Does the Christian faith speak to politics, inequality, injustice, and society? It does, but not from the standpoint of a particular political perspective, political party, or ideology. The only teaching on government involvement by Jesus had to do with giving to Caesar what belongs to Caesar and giving to God what belongs to God. I don't think Jesus was carrying any placards for a candidate in Rome. In other words, Jesus' teaching on politics had more to do with internal transformation, not external domination.

When ideologues use the Bible to proof-text their own religious-political position they are imposing their own political views on the scripture instead of allowing the ancient texts to speak for themselves to the inner kingdom of God that resides in all people.

Making the Bible fit my point of view is the worst biblical interpretation there is. It is a complete misunderstanding of the nature and purpose of the Bible itself. It reduces politicians to using, misusing, and misquoting the Bible on the campaign trail as we saw Donald Trump do in an attempt to quote "Two-Corinthians." It becomes a mockery.

The Religious Rights' program for making America a Christian nation is without substance and grounding. It represents the "Constantinianization" of the American government. The program is designed to primarily pass some laws, overturn others, and enforce Christian principles. It forces everyone to pay homage to their version of Christianity. It includes some of the following oversimplified solutions:

1. Put prayer back in public schools and require bible readings. This they say will solve a host of social problems.

2. End abortion by overturning *Roe v. Wade*, and this will cleanse American culture.

3. End gay marriage through reversing recent court decisions and the traditional family will once again be protected and enshrined as the ideal.

4. Make sure everyone says "Merry Christmas" during the holiday season so that no one forgets that it is about the birth of Christ.

5. Don't let more non-Christian types into the country so that the already majority Christian (white) population will grow and stay in control.

6. Take public money from public education and use it to fund pri-

vate-religious schools that have a religious mission in the name of religious freedom.

7. Build a border wall so that immigrants, who may not be Christians, can't sneak into the U.S. and take jobs, and use up our resources.

8. Do away with the ridiculous notion that all religions are equal in the U.S. To be sure, all religions are allowed, but the unofficial-official one is Christianity.

That is the program of the religious right. It dumbs down the whole process of truly understanding what transformation means. The perspective that the Kingdom of God is somehow a politically based, legal power structure makes the solution a completely external one. There is no need for internal faith and transformation. And it can only be implemented through religious and political coercion.

It is reminiscent of the Constantinian solution that came into being in 312 when the emperor made Christianity a legal religion. Then Constantine imposed his will on the First Council of Nicaea in 325 and an unholy alliance of Church and State was born. The impact on the Christian religion was severe and it diluted the church.

Jesus did teach about the "Kingdom of God," but it doesn't take a shrewd observer to realize that this concept was not an earthly one or a political one. Jesus said clearly, "the kingdom of God is within you." The battlefield is internal, within each of us. Faith is necessary to overcome the worst inclinations of our soul especially in a politician. It relates to Jesus' teaching about "taking the log out of your own eye." Not pointing out the speck in your enemy's eye.

Political power in the hands of a person that has never connected with the kingdom of God within themselves is a dangerous individual. Lack of connection and understanding of one's own interior life is to be disconnected from the Kingdom of God. It isn't about external political power or outward religious affiliation, but it is all about internal spiritual connection and understanding leading to self-awareness, compassion, empathy and sacrifice.

Using politics to advance a religious agenda is a gross distortion of Christ's teachings, spirituality, and the Christian faith. The place of faith in the political sphere is to provide internal grounding, connection, and life to those that hold political power. This is the only antidote to the corrupting influence of political power. Those that think they will bring the faith to political office are sadly mistaken if they think that faith is a political manifesto. The only thing they are promoting is another form of religious-political authoritarianism or Constantinianism.

How does interior connection and faith impact how leaders approach politics? I think it begins to turn on its head the traditional options that we have been thinking about.

First, it is much more difficult than the religious right agenda because faith and internal grounding is hard work, soul searching hard work. For example, bringing interior faith and spirituality to politics:

1. means that a politician is governed by an internal core of being, not the influence of ideologues, bankers, corporate leaders, and other corrupt influences,

2. means that a leader is whole personally and governs by the integrity of their own soul. They cannot be bought or sold,

3. means that faith strengthens the resolve of a leader to do what's right to the benefit of all Americans, particularly the powerless and marginalized,

4. means that a leader, whether they pray, meditate, or otherwise spend time reflecting, finds guidance and direction from an interior compass to make critical decisions,

5. means that a leader sees the big picture, and not a parochial issue. For instance, they focus on how policy can create an environment where all loving couples can thrive and where families are encouraged and supported, regardless of sexual orientation,

6. means that a political leader will have to make unpopular decisions that lead to a loss of support sometimes. It means decisions are not made in their own best interest,

7. means they focus on helping create the conditions where every expectant mother has the support, medical care, and economic means to decide what is best for the human life they are carrying, and hopefully they will feel the empowerment to choose life,

8. means they can focus on providing a system to promote the health and wellbeing of all people that provides adequate care for all people regardless of their means,

9. means they aren't focused on "sticking it to the rich" through taxation but are interested in creating a just system that supports the needs of those that cannot take care of themselves and provide meaningful work for those that are able,

10. and that the most important factor in the inner Kingdom of God, is not to be worried about whether I am right or wrong politically, but whether I am loving my neighbor as I love myself. This is transformative politics.

Connecting with the "Christ narrative" within our soul transforms priorities. Politics without grounding internally becomes a silly pastime but politics grounded in an inner faith results in connecting with people and solving problems.

The Religious Right wants to turn the United States into a Christian Nation which would result in a quasi-theocratic Republic. But another alternative could be if political leaders were to govern based on the teachings of Christ in the Sermon on the Mount. I wonder what the result could be? To this point in history, it has never been tried.

SIXTEEN

HOW END-TIMES THEOLOGY RUINS LIVES AND THREATENS OUR FUTURE

I grew up with great fear that I had missed the rapture whenever my parents were not home. My dad as a minister, had a 24-hour prayer hotline. During the days of my rebelling, if my parents were missing, I often would call the prayer hotline. As long as someone answered, I felt relieved that the rapture had not come, so I would just hang up. I am 54-years-old now, and until probably 7 or 8 years ago, I was certain that I was damned to hell. Today, I believe in a god or higher power, but I am not a Christian. If there is ever going to be a judgment day, I believe that I will be judged for how I lived my life, not on what organized religion that I am affiliated with.[1]

—Troy Huelle

In 1970 when I was a sophomore in High School, I picked up a copy of Hal Lindsay's new book entitled, *"The Late Great Planet Earth."* Being a flaming Jesus Freak at that time I was enthralled with this modern interpretation of end time Biblical passages and prophecy, and I swallowed every word of it. His book read like a novel as he predicted end time events leading up to the "rapture of the church" and the beginning of the reign of the Antichrist. I loved it and felt like I had some special inside knowledge about the future and even started a discussion group in the school's library study room where I shared these imaginations with my friends, some of whom thought I was crazy, but others found them to be credible.

End Time Teaching in Popular Media

At about the same time the song *"I Wish We'd All Been Ready"* was released by the original Christian rocker, Larry Norman. (Also wrote, *"Why Should The Devil Have All The Good Music")* Whether Norman was inspired by Lindsay's book I can't say, but it contained the same message...Jesus is coming soon to rapture his followers just before "The Great Tribulation" which will last for seven years, and then Christ will return to rule and reign. It will be a time when the world will devolve into violence, chaos, and ruin.

Every self-respecting Christian musician of that era learned this song and sang it *ad infinitum*. I was no exception. At every youth group meeting, coffee house visit or small group prayer meeting we were singing this clarion warning song, "I wish we'd all been ready."

Then, as if on cue in 1972, the film *A Thief In The Night* was released by Don Thompson from Des Moines, Iowa. His movie production company, Heartland Productions, had a budget of $68,000, but over the next 10 years the movie would gross $4.2 million.[2] The film was so successful that a cottage industry of Christian apocalyptic films was created, and three more similar themed small budget films followed. Suddenly, the Christian-horror apocalypse film genre emerged. They were designed to literally "scare the hell out of people." And they did.

The films did what the book and song could not; create a visual-audio sensory experience of what the world would become when Christians are raptured and "the Beast" would rule the world (through the United Nations of course), and you were left behind.

The films depicted a gory and graphic series of persecutions, executions and terror that was targeted against those that are true believers in Jesus Christ. Meant as fiction I think, the faithful evangelical throng that went to experience it didn't take it as such, not by a longshot. The general belief was this is going to happen, soon, and you don't want to be left behind.

All through the 1970's Evangelical revivals at the least included references to the impending Rapture of the Church, and the horrible ordeal people would face if they were left behind. No altar call was complete without "*I Wish We'd All Been Ready*" playing in the background as a preacher called forth repentance and coming to Jesus. The films were shown to countless youth groups, summer camps, Christian schools and any other venue to elicit conversion experiences out of fear. And respond they did, by the thousands.

All this media and music pre-dates the even more successful *Left Behind* series (2000, 2002, 2005) which was more professionally produced and even utilized known Hollywood actors, although film criticism was still universally negative. These films would have a similar and even more profound impact on the next generation of young Christian minds. However, *A Thief In The Night* led the way and prepared the evangelical mind with these images, doctrines and a healthy dose of fear and dread.

Why This Matters Today

Those Jesus Freaks that grew up on a diet of this end-time apocalyptic messaging are now in their 50's, 60's and 70's and are still affected by the images, horror and trauma that this teaching inspired.

I'm not trying to be hyperbolic by using the word "trauma." Many of the young people at the time lived in a constant state of fear and anxiety. It was real. Many reported nightmares and coming home to empty houses and worrying that the rapture had taken place and their parents were gone. For some this impact has had a residual effect even to today. More on this in a moment.

The reason this trip back in time is relevant is what is happening now, and for our future. *Back to the Future,* so to speak. There are two outcomes that I think are important to focus on to show the current impact of "end-time" theology. They are the personal-emotional impact they had on a whole generation of young people, myself included. And second, their political impact as seen today in the highest reaches of the federal government, where many of the people that are making policy and running government institutions have carried these doctrines and ideas into their work.

Beliefs about biblical prophecy and end times can be clearly seen as a straight line from Hal Lindsay's 1970 book, through *A Thief In the Night* to the *Left Behind* series, right down to current policy makers. The impact and implications are perhaps more frightening than the end time predictions themselves.

The Personal Toll

First, the psychological and emotional impact. To say that exposing kids to these types of images and movies is borderline neglect and abuse is not an exaggeration. While most parents, especially religious parents, are vigilant about what types of shows and movies their kids consume, the "Rapture" movies were an exception, because they saw them as a way to "scare the hell" out of their children and bring them to Christ. Many of the young people, now adults, have reported over the years extreme anxiety, depression, and fear that they still deal with today. Here are some of the comments that you can find through Twitter or Facebook; I've left the names out for anonymity:

"I was very afraid the rapture might occur and I might be left behind. One morning when I was ten or twelve I woke up and couldn't find anyone in the house. Before I realized that my mom and siblings had simply gone outside to enjoy the beautiful morning, I completely freaked, convinced that the rapture had occurred and I had been left behind. That fear was real and palpable."

"Woke up many nights when it was silent, thinking my family got raptured, to have to sneak down the hall to peek in on my sister to see if she was still in her bed. It was nightmarish and scary, and I hated it."

"We were post tribulationists. I had plans, where would I run with my siblings, as the oldest, I figured my parents would maybe be able to stall the authorities long enough for me to get the rest of us gone. We'd hide until we were finally caught and tortured until we either died or recanted faith and went to hell."

"One day during a chapel service, the school admin orchestrated a group of men in camo fatigues to barge in, declare that the one world government had formed, that Christianity was illegal now and we were all being arrested."

"I never knew where most of my anxiety and depression came from. This all makes sense."

"I spent my childhood terrified of being left behind. I am told I accepted Jesus in my heart at 4; it didn't matter though.

I would still pray the sinner's prayer often just in case the rapture happened. I never felt safe."

"I came home from school when I was six years old and no one was home. I experienced major panic and rapture anxiety. This scenario isn't unique. It's heartbreaking that we, as children felt we were so terrible/horrible that our Heavenly Father could fathom leaving us behind."

"I'm a 6w5 and was scared of hell as a kid. I'd cry in my room begging God to save me from hell. Omgosh . . . I've had rapture anxiety as an adult, and I thought I was being crazy and ridiculous and legit stupid. I had no idea this was a thing!!"

"In my church we were taught the rapture would result in chaos & multi-car pileups because people would be raptured from behind the wheel while driving & their vehicles left behind."

"And all the teenagers were thinking, "Gee, I really hope the rapture doesn't happen before I get to have sex," but we're afraid to say that out loud. It's such a twisted way to grow up."

"Imagine growing up thinking that at any moment, you would cease to exist. You'd just vanish, forced to abandon your life and everything you loved. And you were supposed to be happy about it."

"It's entirely possible that I still have nightmares about the rapture happening and being left behind, etc. religious trauma is real and devastating."

> "My first fundie pastor was obsessed with the Rapture coming in his lifetime, and constantly preached about all the evident signs of the End Times. I remember having nightmares about it. I remember sitting on our stairs begging God to hold off 'til I was older."

These comments are just a small sample reflecting real life experiences that young people who are now adults have had to deal with. The trusted people in their lives; parents, youth leaders, pastors, Christian school teachers or just their friends, told them the Rapture was real and they saw the movies. Internalizing these messages was devastating.

Yet this abusive message continues to be preached to exploit young people into "a relationship with Christ." Many people cite this type of abuse as one of the many reasons they have left evangelical Christianity as my former student said. But even after severing ties to their fundamentalist past the trauma continues to haunt them.

It is no coincidence that Christian end-time teaching resurges periodically in relation to societal change and turbulence. The release of *Late Great Planet Earth* came in the wake of the violence and social upheaval of the 1960's. It was an era when traditional values and social roles were questioned and massive changes in social relationships emerged.

As we entered the 21st Century, again social change was paramount on people's minds. Biggest among these is the growing diversity of American society. It was clear that white Protestants were a shrinking majority and their place in the power structure of society is weakening.

In addition, 9/11 had a clear impact on the American psyche as it appeared that Americans were vulnerable to terrorist attacks from an opposing religious force, Islamism. It was fertile ground for a resurgence of Christian apocalyptic media.

Now again in the 2020's, with the pandemic and social unrest, it is no wonder many are turning to biblical stories and fiction about the apocalypse. But the emotional impact on the vulnerable is severe. Anxiety, panic attacks and depression could be associated not only with these events but in evangelical circles with the end-times scenarios that are continuing to emerge.

It is important to remember that this type of thinking permeates to a deep subconscious level. This is a realm of imagery, symbols, metaphor, emotion, instinct, and primal needs. Nature and nurture then merge into a template for viewing the world which filters every experience. People build an alternative reality where fear and dread rule the emotions.

The Political Impact

Beyond the personal toll that this extremist teaching has taken there is also a political policy threat today. Since the 1980s Christian fundamentalists have pushed further and further into the realm of public life and politics bringing with them the "end times" theology.

Under the Trump administration, it was accurate to say that Evangelical influence was at its zenith in the halls of power. And those religious figures that surrounded Trump, even though he shows no proclivity toward anything religious, are motivated by the same apocalyptic vision of the future that has been portrayed in the movies and books I've mentioned. And this influence has dire consequences. Those that were advising the President whispered these ideas into his ear:

> Jesus may come again at any time, so even if you believe that climate change is real, it doesn't matter. Jesus will make a "new heaven and a new earth" so the climate will be healed by God. Why spend billions on a "green new deal" for something that won't matter.

Jerusalem is the biblical capital of the Jewish state and it was prophetic that it would become the center of a restored Jewish homeland. Recognize it as Israel's capital and fulfill biblical prophecy. You are the chosen one to do this since no other President has had the guts to do it. Never mind that this will forestall peace in the Middle East; make the Arab countries angry and risk an outbreak of war; that is also part of the biblical prophecy.

A world-wide conflict will take place in the Middle East between Iran and Israel. This is inevitable and is prophesized in the Bible and this will usher in the return of Christ, so the sooner that war takes place the sooner we will see our Christ glorified. War is not to be avoided but welcomed.

The globalists are actually preparing the way for the Antichrist and a one-world government that is inspired and controlled by Satan. The U.S. should become isolationist, reject any United Nations initiatives and projects, and put the needs of this country before any other country or governmental entity. Remember, globalists (i.e., democrats and liberals) are evil and are the enemy not only of the country, but of God.

All institutions are to be under the control of God's people. This will prepare the world for the rule of Christ after the Tribulation. They are to dominate government, education, entertainment, media and the economy. Therefore the U.S. government, which was designed to be a Christian Republic, needs to pass and enforce laws that enshrine biblical values and teachings. You should oppose godless, humanistic values and practices. Being an American patriot is one and the same

> with being a good Christian. The government should favor the Christian religion and breakdown the so-called 'wall of separation' that keeps the government from allowing Christianity to dictate the rules.

Who were these Trump whisperers? **Paula White**, who led the prayer at Trump's inauguration and was the chair of the Trump Evangelical Advisory Board. **Robert Jeffress,** also a member of Trump's Evangelical Advisory Board, but is also the pastor of the First Baptist Church of Dallas. **Jerry Falwell Jr**., President of Liberty University in Virginia, the foremost evangelical university in the US. And last but not least, **Franklin Graham**, son of the famous evangelist Billy Graham. Graham suggested opposition to Trump was the work of a "demonic power." He clearly has cast his support and destiny with the Trump administration and justified it partially through end-time doctrine.

Here's a list of some of other key evangelical leaders who were on President Donald Trump's campaign evangelical executive advisory board and have served in an advisory role since his inauguration:

Gary Bauer — president, American Values; former president of Family Research Council; former chief domestic policy adviser in the Reagan administration

Mark Burns — co-founder and CEO of The NOW Television Network in Easley, S.C.; spoke at the 2016 Republican National Convention

Tim Clinton — president, American Association of Christian Counselors

James Dobson — author, psychologist and host, "Family Talk"

Jordan Easley — pastor of Englewood Baptist Church in Jackson, Tenn.; chairs Southern Baptists' Young Leaders Advisory Council

Ronnie Floyd — author and senior pastor, Cross Church in northwest Arkansas; former Southern Baptist Convention president

Jack Graham — author and pastor of Prestonwood Baptist Church in Plano, Texas; former Southern Baptist Convention president

Rodney Howard-Browne — co-founder of The River at Tampa Bay Church and Revival Ministries International in Florida

Harry Jackson — senior pastor, Hope Christian Church in Beltsville, Md.; co-founder of The Reconciled Church: Healing the Racial Divide

Richard Land — president, Southern Evangelical Seminary in Matthews, N.C.; former president, Southern Baptist Convention Ethics and Religious Liberty Commission

Greg Laurie — author and senior pastor of Harvest Christian Fellowship in Riverside, Calif.

Eric Metaxas — author and host, "The Eric Metaxas Show"; speaker, 2012 National Prayer Breakfast

Johnnie Moore — author, religious freedom advocate and public relations executive; serves as unofficial spokesman for group of evangelicals advising Trump administration

Frank Page — president and CEO, Southern Baptist Convention Executive Committee; former Southern Baptist Convention president; former member of President Obama's Advisory Council on Faith-based and Neighborhood Partnerships

Tony Perkins — president, Family Research Council

Ralph Reed — founder, Faith and Freedom Coalition; former executive director, Christian Coalition

Tony Suarez — executive vice president, National Hispanic Christian Leadership Conference

These and many others are of the evangelical-fundamentalist belief in the rapture and second coming of Christ. They have pushed and influenced President Trump to enact policies that favor their religious ideology and book of Revelation machinations.

It is easy to see that in some areas, they have been quite successful. Evangelical leaders didn't support Donald Trump because he is a religious paragon of virtue, but because he listens to them, and enacts policies that they believe will "hasten the return of the Lord."

What about those within the administration that had closer proximity to the President and perhaps more influence on his actions and thinking? They would include the likes of:

Mike Pence: Former Vice President, former Governor of Indiana. Pence is a self-proclaimed "born-again Catholic." He is a major supporter of Israel as much for religious reasons as for any geo-political strategy. In 2009, before the convention of AIPAC, he said: "*Let me say emphatically, like the overwhelming majority of my constituents, my Christian faith compels me to cherish the state of Israel.*"[3] Pence also has a strong belief in the notion that God will in fact make him President one day. For him this is a conviction of religious belief, not a political objective.

Mike Pompeo: Former Secretary of State and former CIA director for the Trump administration and a self-proclaimed Presbyterian Evangelical. Pompeo has a strong sense of the "end-times" and because of that strongly supported Trump's decision to move the US Embassy to Jerusalem. Pompeo told the American Israel Public Affairs Committee: "*As secretary of state and as a Christian, I'm proud to lead American diplomacy to support Israel's right to defend itself.*"[4] He seems to easily move between his own religious beliefs and foreign policy initiatives, blurring the line between the two.

He certainly believes in the "Rapture" of the church, the chosen ones. "*We will continue to fight these battles,*" he said at a "God and Country Rally" in 2015, because there is a "*never-ending struggle*" until "*the rapture.*" For Pompeo's audience, the rapture invoked an apocalyptic Christian vision of the future, a final battle between good and evil, and the second coming of Jesus Christ, when the faithful will ascend to heaven and the rest will go to hell.

William Barr: Former Attorney General for the Trump Administration and devout Catholic. He is known to oppose the concept of the separation of church and state. In a telling speech that he gave at the University of Notre

Dame Law School, he declared: "*. . . the force, fervor, and comprehensiveness of the assault on religion we are experiencing today. This is not decay; it is organized destruction. Secularists, and their allies among the "progressives," have marshaled all the force of mass communications, popular culture, the entertainment industry, and academia in an unremitting assault on religion and traditional values.*"[5]

Barr, although not overtly evangelical, still sees the forces of good vs. evil working within all institutions, and divides citizens into those that favor good, the religious, and the evil "progressives." This plays perfectly into an end-time vision of good-evil confrontation.

There were many others within that administration that were driven by "biblical religious conviction" and saw no conflict in inserting those convictions into public policy and debate.

But the real danger comes in the arena of foreign policy as these end-time advisors continued to whisper in Trump's ear the apocalyptic message of the book of Revelation, where many evangelicals believe Iran plays a special and specific role.

Diana Butler Bass who has studied the history of fundamentalism in America made this observation: "When Iran gets into the news, especially with anything to do with war, it's a prophetic dog whistle to evangelicals. They will support anything that seems to edge the world towards this conflagration," she says. "They don't necessarily want violence, but they're eager for Christ to return and they think that this war with Iran and Israel has to happen for their larger hope to pass."[6]

It's not hard to see how apocalyptic Evangelicalism influenced the Trump administration as it sought to mobilize the millions of Evangelicals reached by televangelists and megachurch pastors preaching the End Times. And just because Trump was defeated in the 2020 election, the Evangelical religious right is still there, still active, and should another Trump-type President assume office, we will be right back where we were in 2016!

Personal Note

Having fled the Evangelical community since the early 2000s, one of the more refreshing and cleansing experiences I've had is to shed the worry and anxiety about the so-called rapture and chaos of the Great Tribulation. For me, it is enough to see such suffering and violence taking place on a daily basis, but to know that over the stretch of time of human history our situation has actually improved; and violence, warfare and crime have all actually declined and are at their lowest levels of any time in human history. Optimism of this sort in humanity's future was forbidden by end-times theology. Things had to be getting worse because that was always the sign of the times. But it has been refreshing for me to be able to embrace the wonderful idea that humans can indeed improve life for billions of people, seek peaceful solutions for conflicts and reduce hunger, ignorance and poverty for people all over the planet. We do not need a second coming of Christ to improve our human community. And that for me, is the sweetest message I can now preach.

Seventeen

ONCE UPON A TIME BEFORE EVANGELICALS WERE REPUBLICANS

> A large bus and several cars with Jesus painted on the side roll into the Houghton—Hancock area. Thirty—six freaky—looking kids spill out onto the streets. The girls with ankle—length dresses and long—haired boys fortified with armloads of [Jesus] papers scatter and start rapping with the closest passerby . . .[1]
>
> —**Houghton-Hancock Newspaper**, 1972

Once upon a time, in a land before computers, cable TV, and the Rush Limbaugh show, there was a time when Christians were not automatically Republicans. GASP! I warn you this is a frightening tale. Read on if you dare.

IF you came of age in the 1980s there were certain cultural and religious assumptions that you simply acquired by osmosis. One of those assumptions was that all Evangelicals were Republicans and voted for Ronald Reagan. By 1980, and certainly by 1984, the embryo of Evangelical political awareness had grown into a full-blown political identity with conservatism and the Republican Party.

The champions of Evangelical politics were everywhere. Jerry Falwell led the Moral Majority, Pat Robertson, the Charismatic Christian Television prophet, ran for President and placed well in the Iowa Caucuses in 1988.

Other names like Ralph Reed with the Christian Coalition, and James Dobson, who founded the "Focus on the Family" ministry, emerged as fund-raising, Bible-believing political organizers on behalf of "family values" candidates. And, perhaps the strongest advocate-organizer of the Christian right was Paul Weyrich who, along with several others, founded *the Heritage Foundation* as a right-wing Christian think-tank to develop policies and ideas that fed the Christian right movement.

By 1990, it was simply a given that if you were a true Bible-believing Christian, then you would most certainly support candidates like George Bush (both of them), and other candidates for high office such as Pat Robertson, and later on Mike Huckabee or Rick Santorum. Conservatism was interchangeable with the "good news." Lower taxes, increased defense spending, cutting social programs and praising the lord.

This is what makes it so ironic that a man such as Barack Obama who wrote about, talked about, and integrated a Biblical view of life into his own political ideology, was roundly condemned and scorned by those on the Christian Right, simply because he was considered a liberal. I'll leave the heritage of white nationalism out of the equation at this point but suffice it to say that the religious right had no use for a person of faith if they were not conservative by the 2000s.

It is no coincidence then, that the election of 2016 witnessed the mass movement of Evangelicals (81%) into the camp of Donald Trump, who by his own admission, needs no forgiveness from anyone including God. It is a strange alliance but simply proves that political identity, which became part and parcel of Evangelicalism in the 1980s has now absorbed the former movement and has stripped the term "Evangelical" of any true spiritual meaning. The mutation is now complete. Evangelicals are now Republicans first, and the good news is a faint afterthought.

Such is the nature and way that political power tends to absorb all that is around it, distorts any message of spirituality in the name of power, and allows people that call themselves "bible believers" to accept a man as President that is a self-proclaimed sex predator, adulterer, race baiter and cheat when it comes to his own business concerns.

If you grew up in the 1980s, as many of my former history students did, you might not realize that there was a time, long-long ago, when Evangelicals didn't identify themselves as conservatives or Republicans or in many cases, with any political ideology. They might not realize that in the annals of modern Evangelical history many Evangelical leaders of the past were either indifferent to politics or ran a course in the middle such as Billy Graham, trying to provide a biblical influence on both parties and any President regardless of their ideology.

There were many Evangelicals that would have been considered liberal. Yes, I know this creates a certain level of cognitive dissonance but let me take you back in time.

Speaking of coming of age, I went through that passage around the late 1960's. After the 1963 assassination of JFK, I became politically aware that there's *"something happening here, but what it is ain't exactly clear."*

Coming of age during one of the most tumultuous periods of modern time was indeed confusing for a young person in their teens. But I did have the advantage, as I see it now, of being grounded in an Evangelical church. This church preached a clear gospel of love and good news to all people, and though it tended to resist many of the social changes that were occurring in the 1960's, it did provide an anchor of sorts to me and many of my friends that were searching for meaning and purpose in a period of extreme conflict and hostility. We became what we proudly exclaimed in that time to be Jesus

People. We were one more layer in the broader social movement away from the 1950's and the rigid social norms of segregation, unquestioned authority, defined sex roles, and other injustices of that time.

We viewed Jesus as counter-cultural and revolutionary in message. The message was much more cultural than it was political.

What is so memorable now is that for me and my colleagues of that Jesus freak era, being a Christian had little to do at all with politics. Consider in 1968 there was no *Moral Majority*, no *Focus on the Family*, no *Family Research Council*, no *Heritage Foundation*, no Christian television networks, no conservative talk radio, and no Christian Right. None of these powerful organizations and institutions existed.

The Jesus People that I associated with did curious things such as attend anti-war rallies, march for an end to racial discrimination, advocate for women's equality, and even spoke out in defense of the American Indian Movement (google it).

We accepted interracial marriage at a time when black/white couples were still forbidden to marry in some states. We talked about alternative forms of families before gay marriage was even mentioned. The only thing that seemed important to Jesus freaks was applying the radical love message of Jesus Christ to whatever cultural-social ill afflicted society and the individuals within that system.

We spoke out against poverty which seemed to have an objective of deliberately keeping humans subject to the cruel cycle of low wages, poor education, and unequal opportunity. We didn't know it, but we were quite liberal as were many Evangelical churches. But our interpretation of these beliefs was not through a prism of political ideology but only through the life and teachings of Jesus Christ.

We didn't believe what we believed because it was liberal, we advocated those positions because they were consistent in our minds with the gospel of Jesus Christ. This is a critical distinction.

It might have been that I was raised in a Democratic household. My Iowa farm family were Roosevelt Democrats. They voted for FDR, Harry Truman, John F. Kennedy, and Lyndon Johnson. Barry Goldwater was considered a nutcase and Richard Nixon was already identified by my grandfather as a crook as early as 1960 when he ran for President the first time. So, my own political affinity may have clearly been determined simply by family upbringing.

The broader point is I never made any connection between being a Roosevelt Democrat to being a Jesus freak. Those two labels had no connection. Being a follower of Jesus was not a political consideration. We didn't categorize people religiously based on their political affiliations.

If you were a Republican, you could still be a Jesus freak, and if you were a Democrat, you could still come to the coffee houses and bible studies. No one really cared. All we cared about was loving people regardless of their status, race or position in society and sticking it to the establishment. (I had to get that in.)

When the 1970's came along, and my own political consciousness began to mature along with my Evangelical ideals it seemed easy for me to vote for Jimmy Carter in 1976. That was the first election where I was old enough to vote and I did vote for Carter. The Baptist-Sunday School Teacher-President was a natural fit for me. Carter was clearly not a conservative but for many like me his genuine faith and trust in God were evidence that his ideology would be shaped by an ethical ideal of love. President Carter was the last Democratic candidate to receive over 50% of the evangelical vote.[2]

That is why by 1980 when Ronald Reagan ascended to the Presidency it was a bit of a shock to my own view of Christianity that many of my Christian School colleagues came out in rabid support of him not because he was a Christian (he was a nominal Presbyterian at best), but because he was conservative. Something had happened between 1976 and 1980 and again, it wasn't totally clear what it was. It seemed by 1980 one's Evangelical credentials were determined much more by one's conservative political positions.

Somehow, the thought that my political positions needed to be conservative to be true to my spiritual ideals was like living in a foreign land. I didn't quite get it, but to my own shame over time I began to drink the Kool-Aid. By the mid to late 1980's I started to read and accept, at least on the surface, the evangelical-conservative ideological mixture that made it unacceptable to be a liberal or progressive.

The godless philosophies of humanism and secularism were now the enemies and for a few years I waged battle. I taught my students a Christian Worldview which was actually a conservative ideology sprinkled with religious powdered sugar.

I protested abortion, gay rights and any other liberal cause as if I were praising God-almighty in the process. I railed against welfare and the lazy poor who, according to scripture, should not eat if they didn't work. I supported conservative candidates because they were conservative, not because they expressed any true conviction for social justice or inclusion. Lower taxes, especially on the wealthy, was the new gospel good news.

Part of this was to get along within the Christian School culture that I was committed to and to put bread on my family's table. To rock the boat would certainly put my job at risk and to even become the object of scorn or investigation. It was one of those times in life where you "go along to get along." But it was so uncomfortable and disconcerting, and I could not bring myself to be dogmatically conservative though I tried.

I always hedged and gave room for alternative views within my history classroom. I even had students that would come to me and ask, "Are you really a conservative?" as if it were an inquisition about questions of ultimate faith. My answer was simply "what do you think?" An artful dodge, yes, but also it was a vague declaration that my faith would not be determined by political ideology. I always felt proud to get that question.

Since the 1990's, I have slowly worked my way back from the abyss of conservative-nationalistic-Christianity. By the election of 2004 in the wake of 9/11, it was clear that I could no longer support a conservative, Evangelical candidate like George W. Bush.

In many ways, I have come full circle, although today I would no longer even call myself an Evangelical because that term has lost its meaning. It has taken a long time to undo the effects of the Kool-Aid of conservative-religious right-wing fanaticism, but now that I have rejected the deadly connection between conservative political thought and evangelical Christianity, it feels so right. I have had to reject and expel both Evangelicalism and conservatism.

Not all will feel that way or need to do so. But for me, I have returned to a place where I am able to let my own spiritual ideals determine what my political inclinations are and not the other way around.

So, there you have it. Once there was a place and time where being a Christian didn't mean selling your soul to the conservative movement for power and pride. May it be that we will make it so once again.

EIGHTEEN

THREE EVANGELICAL IDEAS THAT THREATEN THE UNITED STATES

Christian nationalism—the belief that America is God's chosen nation and must be defended as such—serves as a powerful predictor of intolerance toward immigrants, racial minorities, and non-Christians. It is linked to opposition to gay rights and gun control, to support for harsher punishments for criminals, to justifications for the use of excessive force against black Americans in law enforcement situations, and to traditionalist gender ideology.[1]

—**Kristin Kobes Du Mez**, *Jesus and John Wayne*

THERE ARE THREE IDEAS in Evangelical Christianity that have converged in the past 30 years to result in a violent attack at the nation's Capital on January

6, 2021. And these ideas continue to threaten the Democracy of the United States.

They include beliefs in the supernatural world of angels and demons that constantly combat each other and have an impact in the physical world; the toxic masculinity cult; and the extreme gun rights movement. I'll outline how all three of these ideas came into mainstream Evangelical culture and thinking and show how the combination of the three has led to a dangerous and violent mass movement of religiously inspired zealots with guns.

Blurring Spiritual-Physical Warfare

During my Sunday School days back in the 1960's, we sang "*Onward Christian Soldiers*" complete with a pretend march and actions to mimic a real army. While it was fun and helped to get wiggly kids to be engaged for most of it, we saw it for what it was. A metaphor. Of course, we didn't know that word at that time, but we understood that being a Christian didn't really mean carrying a gun and fighting physically with others. That was made clear.

What we also didn't know at the time was the history of the Crusades and other wars of Religion where it wasn't a metaphor, and Christians did fight and kill those that were unbelievers or in some cases, just non-white. It was carried out under the banner of Christ. Singing this song harkened back to those "good ole' days" of Christian armies marching through Europe or the Americas, extinguishing all unbelievers and non-white races.

As I became older as a teen, we held Bible studies and read passages of scripture about "spiritual warfare" like this one from Ephesians 6:10–17:

> *Finally, be strong in the Lord and in the strength of his might. Put on the whole armor of God, that you may be able to stand against the wiles of the devil. For we are not contending against flesh and blood, but against the principalities, against the powers, against the world rulers of this present darkness, against the*

spiritual hosts of wickedness in the heavenly places. Therefore take the whole armor of God, that you may be able to withstand in the evil day, and having done all, to stand. Stand therefore, having girded your loins with truth, and having put on the breastplate of righteousness, and having shod your feet with the equipment of the gospel of peace; besides all these, taking the shield of faith, with which you can quench all the flaming darts of the evil one. And take the helmet of salvation, and the sword of the Spirit, which is the word of God.

Any reasonable person with a spit of common sense will understand these verses paint a word picture, again, a metaphor. Not one of us ever talked about these verses in a literal sense to justify violence and certainly not gun violence. But the word picture itself uses military allusions. It equates "spiritual warfare" with "physical warfare."

Then in the 1980's, Frank Peretti's book of Christian fiction *This Present Darkness* became a Christian bestseller. *This Present Darkness* was Peretti's first published novel for adults and showed a new more contemporary view on angels, demons, prayer, and spiritual warfare as demons and angels interact and struggle for control of the citizens of the small fictional town of Ashton.

It sold more than 2.5 million copies worldwide and remained on the *Christian Booksellers Association* top best sellers list for over 150 consecutive weeks after its release.[2] Copies flew off the shelves and young people of that era were enthralled and entertained by the images of warfare between angels and demons. It was a violent image.

The book created a believable narrative of how angels and demons affect the physical world, and how believers can influence the outcomes of these "spiritual battles" through prayer and "intercession." The line between the spiritual and physical became quite blurred.

Whether you considered the book a good or bad piece of literature, terrible or spot on theology or just a simple horror story, the book did create an "evangelical panic" that saw Satanic forces everywhere in the form of "territorial demons." A movie critic with a fundamentalist background, Dustin Cox, put it this way:

> To this day, evangelical politics are entangled with the idea that demons are literally hiding behind every tree. Global initiatives like the Paris Accords, for example, are to evangelicals the nefarious work of a global cabal—similar in kind to The Universal Consciousness Society—that seeks to enshrine "one-world government" and to crown the Antichrist. Fundamentalists also interpret reproductive rights as proof of demonic influence designed to damn the entire nation. The list could certainly go on; in the evangelical view, every social concern is ultimately a contest between heaven and hell with human souls as the prize.[3]

Toxic Evangelical Masculinity

This spiritual/military mentality intersects with another toxic thread within the Evangelical movement. That is the extreme "manhood movement" which is simply another name for toxic masculinity and patriarchy. And no Evangelical best-selling book has done more to promote this toxic gender identity than John Eldredge's bestselling book, *Wild at Heart: Discovering the Secret of a Man's Soul.* Christian men were encouraged to model their lives after Mel Gibson's William Wallace from the movie "*Braveheart.*" According to Eldredge, God was a warrior god and men were made in his image.

Pastors played clips of the film in Sunday sermons, Christian men attended weekend *Wild at Heart Boot Camps,* churches organized homegrown

"Braveheart Games," and one Christian college boasted a Braveheart dorm. The imagery and the violence were justified in these teachings and sermons.

The evolution and emergence of this movement is outlined well by Kristin Kobes Du Mez in her recent book, *"Jesus and John Wayne: How White Evangelicals Corrupted the Faith and Fractured a Nation."* Strong masculine images, myths and stereotypes are nothing new to culture and history, but what Du Mez reveals in her book as a New York Times reviewer writes: "'*Jesus and John Wayne*' is a sweeping, revisionist history of the last seventy-five years of white evangelicalism, revealing how evangelicals have worked to replace the Jesus of the Gospels with an idol of rugged masculinity and Christian nationalism—or in the words of one modern chaplain, with "a spiritual badass."[4]

Du Mez goes on to write that Evangelical support for Donald Trump in 2016 and 2020 wasn't just a transactional agreement. Du Mez reveals that Trump in fact represented the fulfillment, rather than the betrayal, of white Evangelicals' most deeply held values: patriarchy, authoritarian rule, aggressive foreign policy, fear of Islam, ambivalence toward *#MeToo*, and opposition to Black Lives Matter and the LGBTQ community. In other words, Trump represented the perfect masculine, Evangelical superhero, a modern-day William Wallace.[5]

Evangelicals didn't support Trump solely because of what they thought he could deliver to them in terms of policies and appointments, but they supported him because of the myth created around him that allows them now to support his most overt lying about the 2020 election, conspiracies like "Q" and ultimately the attempt to force the Congress to abandon its Constitutional duty to count electoral votes on January 6, 2021. More on that in a moment.

Evangelical Radical Gun Culture

The third thread of this trifecta of mental pictures will not be hard to predict. If Evangelicals are driven by a literal militarized view of spirituality and a toxic aggressive masculinity that defies everything that Jesus taught, then absorbing the radical gun culture is an easy next step. It is easy to see how guns have been politicized in the past 30 years, but what may be even more astounding is how guns have been spiritualized.

Over the past few years, a new Christian Youth Conference has emerged out of the Evangelical radical gun movement. Called *Bullets and Bibles*, the "Active Self-Protection Association" advertises their program trying to lure young evangelical students to their summer program. And, not coincidentally at the bottom of their website is a large, ostentatious advertisement for ammo. "*Ammo Shipped Fast*" is guaranteed.

One theme that is communicated throughout the classes and conferences they promote in addition to self-defense and home-defense, is "defense of the vulnerable." It seems that this is where the militarized spiritual world view plus the aggressive masculinity meets the gun culture. The objective is to defend the vulnerable, using firearms. Bible studies are conducted to justify this practice.

Then there is the Alabama car dealer in 2019 that gave away Bibles, guns, and American flags with the purchase of a new or used car.[6] Or, how about the Lt. Governor of Idaho pictured waving a gun and a Bible out of the cab of her pickup in 2020?[7] Going back farther, in 2010 a Michigan gun manufacturer was known to imprint Bible verses in high-powered rifle sights provided to the US military for use in Iraq and Afghanistan.[8]

Faithful Christians can also now go to Amazon and purchase a "Concealed Gun Storage Bible." It is a book with a "Bible" cover, but the inside is a hollowed-out area for concealing a gun. The words of the Bible itself do not appear, but it is a diversion for Christians to secretly carry a gun under the guise of a Bible.

Evangelical gun culture can be seen routinely throughout churches in America and the messages they send. Before Jerry Falwell Jr. was forced to resign from Liberty University due to sexual scandal, he argued for churchgoers and even Christian college students to arm themselves.

Shortly after the 2015 mass shooting in San Bernardino, California, that left 14 people dead and 22 others wounded, then Liberty University President Jerry Falwell Jr. stood before his student body and reached for a gun he claimed to have holstered behind him. "I've always thought if more good people had concealed carry permits, then we could end those Muslims before they walked in," the then-school president said.[9]

Many Evangelical and fundamentalist churches view Kyle Rittenhouse as a hero. The gallant, young masculine male who took up arms to defend property during the Kenosha riot in 2020 is deemed an example of aggressive masculinity. Despite being found not guilty of murder, two people died at the end of his AR 15. Evangelicals praise him for his courage.

Then there is the support for easy gun access. According to the *2018 Cooperative Congressional Election Study*, white Evangelicals and Mormons were the only religious groups who expressed majority support for legislation that would make it easier to obtain a concealed-carry gun permit, with 54.4% and 51.9% saying they would back the idea, respectively.[10]

Michael W. Austin, a professor of philosophy at Eastern Kentucky University and author of *God and Guns in America*, said "I think that there is a unique mix in the United States of faith, patriotism, militarism, self-sufficiency, family and sometimes regional traditions that have led many to think that gun ownership is an essential right, as something that Christians should believe to be central."[11]

Du Mez agrees with Austin, arguing that pro-gun theologies often end up mixing with forms of patriarchy and white supremacy. "For white evangelicals, this image of a strong masculine protector was always a white racial ideal," she said.[12]

Du Mez is correct. White Supremacy has always had a role in this dogma as well. White heavily armed males in the South were considered the patriarchs and protectors of the virtue of white women in the aftermath of emancipation when it was assumed black men would be raping white women. Christian "duty" included terrorizing, tracking down and lynching black men for so much as a look or comment that was "out of line."[13] Strains of white supremacy are still present in this toxic and religious devotion to guns, but it is now also aimed at "communists" and "socialists" as the new threats to Christian purity.

The Assault on the Capitol

This brings us to January 6, 2021. When extreme fanatical religious beliefs are intertwined with militarized spirituality, toxic patriarchy and biblical justifications for using firearms, you can bet something bad is going to happen.

Among the rioters at the Capitol on January 6 were not only Trump supporters but engraved on T-shirts and posters were messages that included: "Jesus is my savior, Trump is my President," or "God, Guns, Trump" and on the sweatshirt of the man constructing the gallows in front of the Capitol, "Faith, Family, Freedom."

Other protesters engaged in rituals such as prayer, casting demons out of Congress, exorcisms and some sang hymns and Christian songs as they ransacked the halls of Congress and beat the Capitol police senselessly.

Setting the stage for the January 6 attack was the earlier December 12 "*Jericho March*" which brought together a number of religious right factions to imitate the biblical Battle of Jericho in prayer to "bring down the walls of the Deep State."

The event featured an odd array of charismatic Evangelicalism, Christian Zionism, and right-wing Catholicism. The event was emceed by Evangelical mega-pastor Eric Metaxas. The week of the Jericho March rally, he told *TurningPoint USA* founder Charlie Kirk that the 2020 election was like "somebody is being raped or murdered ... times a thousand," and that conservatives would need "to fight to the death, to the last drop of blood" to keep Trump in office.[14] So much for spiritual warfare.

Finally, religious studies scholar Jerome Copulsky, co-director of a new website, *Uncivil Religion*, dedicated to collecting digital artifacts of Jan. 6 religiosity says, "It wasn't just the Stop the Steal rally, then the assault. People wanted to display their religious commitments, literally wearing them on their sleeves."[15] These rioters were not trying to hide their motivations. It was transparent and open.

This would not be the first time in history when violence justified in the name of God would threaten society. But at this juncture in American history, Evangelicals are at the vanguard of the demise of a democratic system that has held for over 200 years.

When I left the Evangelical fold in 2005, in addition to many doubts that I have already expressed, I was deeply concerned about these trends that I was seeing even then. In the aftermath of 9/11, and the popularity of the "Left Behind" series I heard from many Evangelicals that the struggle was no longer spiritual, but real. Many young men trying to prove their manliness joined the military to fight in a Holy War against Muslims, despite President Bush admonishing people not to see it that way. Many believed that this was the beginning of the "end-times." The Evangelical movement, already losing touch with reality, was coming off the rails. Donald Trump and Jan. 6 were simply the capstone of this distorted theology.

These trends have been evolving for decades within the Evangelical hot-house culture. Militarized spirituality, toxic masculinity and extreme gun ideology has created a religious battering ram that threatens civil society. It wasn't started by Donald Trump; but as the darling of this toxic brand of religious extremism he has manipulated it for his own gain and support. He or others like him will continue to do so until political leaders and religious leaders hopefully see the danger and put guardrails and stops on this process before something even more destructive takes place, of course . . . in the name of God.

PART FIVE

OTHER DECONSTRUCTION "HERESIES"

NINETEEN

EIGHT REASONS I AM PRO-LIFE

I do not believe that just because you're opposed to abortion that that makes you pro-life. In fact, I think in many cases, your morality is deeply lacking if all you want is a child born but not a child fed, not a child educated, not a child housed. And why would I think that you don't? Because you don't want any tax money to go there. That's not pro-life. That's pro-birth. We need a much broader conversation on what the morality of pro-life is.[1]

—**Sister Joan Chittister**, 2004

NOTHING ENERGIZES THE EVANGELICAL community more than the issue of abortion. Since the 1980s the Evangelical marriage to conservative politicians has placed that issue at the center of the Republican party's priorities. And now that the Supreme Court with a solid conservative majority has gutted abortion rights for women and overturned *Roe v. Wade* completely, conservative-Republican controlled states are passing state laws to ban abortion and criminalize women and doctors.

One of the strategies Evangelicals have used is the zero-sum equation of not allowing someone to be pro-Choice and pro-life at the same time. Because they crouch their argument in terms of "murder" there is no other option but to either be pro-Choice or Pro-Life. You can't be both. At least that is the argument.

What if Pro-Choice doesn't automatically mean Pro-Abortion? Perhaps being pro-Choice means knowing that unsafe abortions took place before laws were in place to make it safer. It means looking for better ways to lower abortion rates than criminalizing women. Why is banning abortion the only option? Thank goodness there will still be many states that preserve and protect a woman's right to choose.

So while declaring myself to be pro-choice, I am also pro-life, 100%, unabashedly pro-life. I believe that every human life is important and sacred. I believe in the principles inherent within the Declaration of Independence that our system should support *"LIFE, liberty and the pursuit of happiness"* and that these rights are endowed upon all people, not just Americans, by virtue of being born.

The same principles that ensure the right to life, liberty and pursuit of happiness must also contain the element of health and bodily autonomy for everyone. In a democratic society there is no place for governmental control and coercion over a woman's body and the decisions she makes with her body. If the government can control someone's bodily autonomy, then no right is safe, ever.

Unfortunately, the label "pro-life" has acquired a narrow definition within our culture and certainly within the Evangelical church. In fact, if there were a single issue that explains the overwhelming support for Donald Trump in the 2016 election, it would be the hope among Evangelicals that a President Trump appoint Supreme Court Justices that will overturn *Roe v Wade*. Never mind the character of the man they would elect to the highest, most powerful office on the planet.

Starting around 1980, being pro-life became a non-negotiable issue within the Evangelical faith. To hedge on this issue, or worse to be a Christian and be pro-choice was considered heretical. Never mind that many Evangelical churches were neutral or even pro-choice in the decade prior to Roe. All of a sudden it was the litmus test for "true Christianity."

The interpretation of what it means to be pro-life in this narrow sense is not in any way life-giving. The pro-life movement has only one objective and one objective only to the exclusion of all other goals. Stop abortions by criminalizing it. In other words, they are pro-birth only.

I was part of this crowd in the 1980's. I accepted the idea that abortion is murder and spent some of my time standing on busy streets holding signs that said as much. I taught my students an uncompromising position on abortion and said there is no middle ground. I taught that you can't be both pro-life and pro-choice. I argued with those that tried to take such a stand, and now, in 2022, I admit I was wrong. Totally, 100% wrong.

I no longer believe being pro-life and pro-choice are opposing viewpoints, if you define what it means to be pro-life in a broad sense. In fact, I would suggest that the life and teachings of Jesus have more to do with matters much broader and more important than the single issue of abortion. And actually, Jesus never said a word about abortion.

There are at least eight ways to think about being pro-life in this comprehensive sense, because once a person declares themselves to be pro-life it is incumbent on that person to be careful how they apply that label and are consistent.

First, to be comprehensively and consistently pro-life means to:

Support Health Care for All Americans

Health care is a right regardless of social class because without proper health care we cannot have a full and happy LIFE. In a country as rich as this one, it is a crime and disgrace to think that we do not have the means to provide adequate; no, outstanding health care for all people. How would it be possible to pursue happiness, liberty, and life, if one does not have access to adequate health care? Making this accessible to all is consistent with our founding principles as well as the life of Christ who healed countless individuals during his earthly ministry. I believe in universal health care for all because I am pro-life.

Support Continued Funding of Planned Parenthood

Planned Parenthood has become the Evangelical-straw-man-punching bag that is blamed for the evil of abortion. But the irony is that the health care services that Planned Parenthood provides, especially to low-income women, enhances the quality of LIFE for these women and families. The majority of Planned Parenthood's clients receive services to prevent unwanted pregnancy. Defunding this organization will only increase the number of unwanted pregnancies resulting in an increase in abortions. It is especially offensive that wealthy men with Cadillac health care insurance policies and fat bank accounts want to defund an organization whose main purpose is to provide basic health services to poor women and families. Planned Parenthood helps to promote LIFE for millions of poor women therefore, I support Planned Parenthood because I am pro-life.

Stop Supporting the Death Penalty

Taking a "life for a life" is an ancient and antiquated form of retributive justice that serves to undermine the principle of life. It is blight on American culture and society that we still tolerate retributive justice over redemptive and restorative justice. Additionally, it is certain that innocent victims have been put to death. Since 1973, more than 160 people have been released from death row with evidence of their innocence.[2] How many innocent victims have perished?

We condemn Middle East countries today that still engage in this medieval form of torturous punishment, yet somehow justify it through some magical interpretation of an ancient text that was written in the same Middle Eastern culture that we now condemn. The death penalty destroys LIFE, so I reject the death penalty because I am pro-life.

Support Regulating the Sale and Ownership of Firearms

Too many innocent people, including children, lose their LIFE due to gun violence in this country to the tune of over 30 people per day. That equates to over 30,000 human lives per year.[3] Since 1999, the number of gun deaths held steady year after year—at 10.4 firearm fatalities per 100,000 people. But in 2015, the rate began creeping up nationwide to 11.8 deaths per 100,00 people–marking a 13.8-percent increase.[4] But more recently, in 2020 there were 45,222 gun-related deaths.[5] Many more than in previous years. How can anyone claim to be pro-life and NOT support the better enforcement of current laws to curb the proliferation of guns, keeping them out of the hands of criminals, rapists, domestic abusers, drug dealers and other nefarious types? I even support the restriction of various classes of guns that have no purpose other than the destruction of LIFE, human life specifically, quickly, efficiently, and amorally. Hiding behind the 2nd Amendment and claiming that criminals will get guns anyway, so there is nothing we can do is anti-life, and it is cowardice. Guns have no other utilitarian purpose other than to end LIFE, and to do so as fast and furious as possible. I am for gun regulations because I am pro-life.

Support Any Efforts, Public or Private, to Reduce Poverty in the U.S. and Around the World

To the question of should the government provide a social safety net for the poor or should it be private charities? I say "YES" to both. It is unacceptable that approximately 70% of America's school children qualify for free or reduced lunch because their family incomes are below the poverty level.[6] That represents about 21 million school children coming from homes that qualify for a free or reduced-price school lunch. And this was pre-covid. The numbers are even higher now.

The middle class is collapsing around us, and we still worry about tax cuts for billionaires. Because I am pro-life, I support all programs that provide basic necessities for the poorest of our citizens: food, housing, medical care, care for disabled, care for our veterans, and jobs.

Support a Living Wage for All Workers

Because I am pro-life, I believe in requiring employers to provide a LIVING wage so that those that do have jobs can experience the LIFE-giving dignity of self-reliance. Supporting a rise in the minimum wage to $15 is a pro-life position. I support any and all efforts to reduce poverty because I am pro-life.

Support Efforts of the U.S. Government to Use Diplomacy, Not War

Being pro-life means supporting the use of diplomacy over war every time the option arises. The war making machine that the U.S. has created and sustains is immoral and has snuffed out LIFE through the propagation of war, arms dealing, encouraging arms races throughout the world, and arming both sides in local or regional conflicts. This is the opposite of pro-life and it is unconscionable that the US spends more on defense than the next 10 nations combined.[7] To be pro-life is to support the idea that the US should at least spend as much on peacemaking and establish a Department of Peace as it does on so-called defense. Of course, war as a self-defensive measure sometimes must happen; but one can hardly classify any of the wars of the past 70 years as truly self-defensive. I support the pursuit of peace making in all situations internationally because I am pro-life.

Support Funding and Innovation to Improve Our Educational System

Nothing in our culture and history has contributed more to LIFE than a superb educational system. It is the second major reason immigrants come to the U.S. after economic reasons. Our educational system is the finest in the world despite the propaganda we have been fed in the religious right media. In every research study conducted, higher educational attainment is positively correlated with better health care reducing health care costs, higher economic achievement to individuals lowering welfare costs, lower incarceration rates reducing prison costs, and overall higher economic growth boosting GDP and wages.[8] More and better education enhances LIFE. Therefore, I support investments in our educational system and finding ways to provide access to college education for ALL people without having to incur crushing economic debt, which kills the quality of LIFE for those burdened under it. Yes, accessible and affordable post-secondary education is a right if we take the Declaration of Independence seriously. I support debt-free college education for any person that wants it because I am pro-life.

Abortion?

Oh wait, did I forget to talk about abortion? No, I didn't forget, but I did intentionally leave it to last for a reason. I will deal with this topic head-on, but you see, a true pro-life position isn't necessarily about abortion only. This in fact might be the least important issue under a broad umbrella of pro-life.

Because I am pro-life, I am against abortion. I would love nothing more than to see all abortions come to an end in this country. Even people that find no moral objections to abortion usually are not out on the street with signs that say, "We Like Abortions, More Abortions, More Abortions." There is a reason for that. This is a difficult decision for any woman to have to make. The process itself I believe does end a life or at least a potential one although identifying when an embryo becomes a "life" is up for scientific discussion. All I know, and I'm not an expert, is that a fetus cannot live on it's own outside of the womb typically any earlier than 24 weeks. Seems to me that at the least, it is a woman's choice up to then.

But this doesn't mean I necessarily believe that outlawing abortion is the right way to end or reduce abortions. And now that abortions are being outlawed in many states in a post-Roe era, the lives of women are at risk in real ways. Outlawing abortion may actually end up being the least pro-life policy there is. There are other proven ways to reduce and even do away with the need for abortions.

In an eight-year period ending in 2017 the State of Colorado saw a 60% drop in the number of abortions performed.[9] Why? It wasn't due to criminalization, but it was due to free access to birth control for all women. Even the number of abortion providers dropped due to a decrease in demand for abortions.

This is the common-sense and most compassionate way to approach this issue. Provide free and easy access to birth control, education, and general health care for all women. Free access to birth control is life-giving and life sustaining.

Now that some states are criminalizing abortion today what will be the result? Will abortion come to an end? Nope, not by a long shot. And every pro-lifer knows this.

Here is what will happen. Women will still seek them out throwing us back to the "good ole days" of back-alley abortions provided by pseudo-doctors with coat hangers and other unsanitary instruments. Women will die from procedures that normally are conducted as an outpatient procedure. This will not promote LIFE. We need to understand this, WOMEN WILL DIE now that abortion is outlawed. Criminalizing abortion or abortion access is the opposite of pro-life. It is pro-death for many women.

Focusing on criminalization of abortion misses the broader issue. Abortion is not the primary problem, but unwanted pregnancy is and the economic and social conditions surrounding a woman seeking an abortion are the issue. The lack of economic, emotional, social, and physical supports many times cause women to see abortion as their only choice.

Women seek abortions not because they want to kill babies, but rather, due to desperate circumstances such as poverty, poor health care, lack of educational opportunity, inadequate food and housing, no or poorly paying jobs, and the list goes on and on. And of course, there are some basic medical reasons that abortions are sometime necessary.

Additionally, the trauma of rape, incest and other violent acts against women are sometimes compounded by an unwanted pregnancy. To not have legal, safe abortion available as an option is cruel and in no way improves the quality of LIFE for many women. To be pro-life is not inconsistent with being pro-choice.

A pro-life position without concern for the quality of life of the child and mother is crass political opportunism at best and morally bankrupt at worse. Many who are self-described pro-lifers are simply pro-birthers. They are only interested in applying some vague interpretation of the Bible that doesn't speak directly to the issue of abortion in the first place, and to use this issue as a wedge political issue to support a generally conservative political agenda. This agenda holds no level of compassion toward the women who are faced with the excruciating moral dilemma and the crushing financial burden of whether to give birth.

Additionally, the Evangelical crusade against abortion usually includes restricting access to safe birth control. That will likely be the next target of the so-called pro-life movement. The purpose of these attempts is to control women's bodies and sexual behavior. Time and again, I hear good religious people say that abstinence is the only form of birth control the Bible condones. Does it?

Opposition to abortion is tied to an Evangelical Patriarchal system that sees women as the "lesser" sex, and bodily autonomy should not be allowed. Decisions about a woman's body should be in the hands of men and politicians no less.

What is interesting is to see how quickly men recoil and oppose any recommendation that perhaps a required vasectomy would end the abortion problem quickly. You can hear shouts of "you can tell me what to do with my body."

I am convinced that we could lower the number of abortions by becoming FULLY PRO-LIFE. Embrace quality of life for all women in all areas, and many of the underlying reasons for abortion will begin to evaporate. When we have a truly loving and caring pro-life movement that encourages all elements of life, then we can consistently and with moral authority work toward the reduction of abortion.

The current pro-life movement is so narrow in its scope and focus that it unwittingly promotes the opposite of what it is seeking: LIFE. To simply end abortion with the stroke of a pen will only lead to more misery and death for many women. It is a cynical and destructive way to try and end the practice of abortion.

I am pro-life, but I want to be consistently and completely pro-life and apply it to the benefit all women and children. Perhaps we need to start a new movement called, the Pro-Quality of Life Movement.

Twenty

WHY CHRISTIANS SHOULD EMBRACE HUMANISM

Sometimes the Bible in the hand of one man is worse than a whisky bottle in the hand of (another)... There are just some kind of men who—who're so busy worrying about the next world they've never learned to live in this one, and you can look down the street and see the results.[1]

—**Harper Lee**, *To Kill a Mockingbird*

One of my all-time favorite movies is "*The Mission.*" It is based on a true account of Jesuit missionaries that attempted time and again to reach out to the remote tribes of the Amazon rainforest to convert them to Christianity, Catholic Christianity to be precise.

The beginning of the movie shows how each of the missionaries that attempted this task was summarily tied to a cross and floated over the edge of a huge waterfall to certain death. It represented a complete rejection of the Christian message along with European civilization with which the religious message was shrouded. Whatever these missionaries were doing to try and convince the tribespeople that they should accept the Christian faith was met with hostility and was considered an insult.

The next Jesuit priest, Father Gabriel, played by Jeremy Irons, makes another attempt to reach this tribe. But this time he doesn't come with bibles, or with preaching or with catechism. He finds a small clearing near the village of the tribe, and simply sits down and plays a flute. Pure simple melodies that appealed to the humanness of these tribal people, who out of curiosity and perhaps lured by the sheer beauty of the music, came out to inspect and see what was going on.

Most accepted him because he appealed to that which was human in them, and then later, they eventually adopted the Christian faith. It is a testament to the power of human-to-human contact and is perhaps the best definition of Christian humanism I've ever seen.

When I was a young Evangelical, I spent most of the time thinking about the afterlife and specifically how to avoid hell and how to get into heaven. This was the prime motivation behind "witnessing" to others.

The Biblical mandate for this effort was the Great Commission to "go into the world and preach the gospel to all nations." So, witness we did. We held Bible studies, music festivals, coffee houses and simply stopped busy people on the street and asked those annoying questions such as "If you were to die tonight, how do you know if you would make it into heaven?" All these efforts and activities were motivated by trying to get people "saved" which meant to us, having assurance of eternal salvation in heaven.

Nothing could tickle our Evangelical little hearts more than a sinner coming home to Jesus and having assurance of life in heaven. Less concern was shown toward what quality of human life they lived thereafter, or the happiness and contribution they might be able to make to other humans around them. Each convert simply became another notch on the baptismal cross representing a soul saved from hell. This appears to me as the same motivation as the missionaries in the Amazon. Reaching out to the tribes to mark a notch on their crucifix.

Later in my journey along the Evangelical path of Christianity, I taught my Christian School students that godless humanism was the enemy that had to be resisted, rejected, and expelled. Humanism was the philosophy that was ruining the very fabric of American culture, so I taught. It was another case of "us vs. them." Humanists were the enemies of God, and to make America pure again, their philosophy had to be expunged.

And so goes the cult of "purity" that permeates Evangelical culture. Purity leaves no room for compassion, which is exactly what humanist philosophy can bring to the table. Theology without compassion is a clanging cymbal, but theology by its nature is purist, exclusive and therefore it divides.

It wasn't until much later as I began deconstructing my prior beliefs that I came to realize that the Christian message is a humanistic one, based on compassion, redemption, and forgiveness. And Jesus is perhaps the greatest of all humanists in history. Scandalous, isn't it?

The misplaced priority of evangelical belief on the afterlife, whatever that is, carries with it certain negative results when applied to this life. When all eyes are on heaven it is easy to miss seeing the injustice and suffering around you. Looking up while walking on a rocky road certainly will cause one to stumble.

Endless debates about the end times and who is in and who isn't bypasses the teachings of Jesus on how to live our lives in the here and now. Compared to his teachings on spirituality and ethics and the proper way to connect with other people, Jesus spent relatively little time saying much of anything about the life hereafter.

Additionally, it can also lead to a rather cynical view of life where the ethical quality and contribution made to others around us is less important than the fact that I'm going to heaven. Eternal salvation becomes the ultimate goal not quality of living.

While the question of eternal salvation and destination after one dies is a question worth discussing for a minute or two, it misses the whole focus and point of the life and teachings of Jesus. It was Jesus who said, *"I have come that you might have life, and life abundant."* Not in the afterlife, but in *this* life.

Following Jesus isn't so much a question of eternal destination but more about your current disposition and the quality of living one is engaged with in the here and now. Faith isn't about the sweet by and by, but it is a key component of being human in the here and now.

To be human is to have faith and to have faith one must connect with the inner life of spirit, the human spirit. In short, perhaps salvation is more about finding and connecting to our own humanity and inner being than it is about anything in the afterlife.

It is no coincidence that a humanist impulse has permeated Christian teaching and theology since the beginning of the Christian religion. Without going into a complete history of Christian humanism, one only needs to look to the book of John to see the kernel and beginning of the fusion of Christian belief with Greek humanism.

The writer of John introduces the divine *logos* or the divine force that underlies and unites the universe and applies it to the life of Christ. The concept of the logos was not new with Christianity but was borrowed from Stoic philosophy of the Greeks.

The second century Christian apologist, Justin the Martyr used this concept to argue that Christian values were consistent with the more ancient notion of divine logos. His argument was meant to connect Christian ethics with secular philosophy giving Christianity more credibility in his day, hence we have the foundations for Christian humanism from the earliest days of the birth of the new religion.

From there throughout the Middle Ages, the Renaissance, Enlightenment, and including today, the Christian message is best understood through a Christo-humanistic lens.

What is a Christian Humanist? The most popular definitions emphasize the humanity of Jesus himself, his social teachings and I would add, his teachings on the inner life, which add to the happiness and fulfillment of being fully human.

It is founded also in the Judeo-Christian teaching of the likeness of God in all people. If all people are born in the image of God, or perhaps more accurately, God born in the likeness of people, then each and every human being has inestimable value and worth. Being human is a high calling and learning to be the most human is the goal.

The concept of incarnation itself is an affirmation of the value of being human that exemplifies itself in the idea of the divine Jesus becoming a person. Incarnation is the ultimate statement of human worth. God becomes human; it is a direct inversion of the priority that many in Evangelical Christianity tend to promote, which is that to be truly godly one must become something other than truly human. Humanity is evil and depraved and to become a Christian is to abandon your own humanity to become something almost superhuman or angelic. But I don't think that's what Jesus taught us.

As Richard Rohr wrote, "Many have said, and I totally agree, that true religion is not trying to make human beings spiritual. We're already spiritual beings. Great religion is trying to make human beings human."[2]

Jesus taught above all how to be human by connecting our faith with our inner life and becoming integrated whole people, human in all aspects. To be spiritual is to be human.

Let me return to the movie, "The Mission." The second part of the movie chronicles the life a totally worldly and ruthless pirate and slave dealer, Rodrigo Mendoza played by Robert DeNiro. Mendoza was vile, mean and without conscience. In a word he was *inhuman*. Mendoza is a great example of people that have no inner connection with their human spirit.

Mendoza falls into a severe depression after killing his half-brother who he found in bed with his fiancé. Although he was acquitted of murder charges Mendoza still wails in depression and seeks absolution for his sins.

That is when the Jesuit Priest, Gabriel (Jeremy Irons), finds Mendoza and proposes a proper penance. He is to carry behind him a shackled bundle of his armor and sword up a steep cliff to the rainforest village where he would then dedicate his life to the service of people who he had previously persecuted.

When the villagers saw him and recognized who he was and witnessed his decrepit and penitent state, they offered redemption and forgiveness to the former slave trader and literally cut away his burden of weight. His bundle of armor and weapons tumbled back down the mountainside. It was one of the most moving Christo-humanistic scenes one could imagine. It had nothing to do with heaven but with complete absolution and redemption in this life.

Mendoza goes on to become a Jesuit priest and ministers to the needs of the villagers. The transformation of Mendoza was one who became fully human through the forgiveness and redemption offered by the "uncivilized" villagers, again showing that spiritual transformation is more about becoming more human.

We can also consider Jesus' Sermon on the Mount, perhaps one of the greatest most poetic teachings on faith and what it means to be fully human in all aspects of our lives. The overriding theme of the Sermon on the Mount is the kingdom of God which Jesus later teaches is within us. Is Jesus actually saying that the kingdom of God is in each of us as we become fully human? I think that this is the point. To break down the Sermon we can start with the beatitudes.

The beatitudes are all about being humble, being peacemakers, being meek, showing mercy, extending compassion and love to others. It is the ultimate **Christo-Humanist Manifesto**. Those that are most human are the most "happy," which is the closest translation of the word "blessed."

The beatitudes stand in stark contrast to the brutish culture of 1st Century Rome and the backcountry of Palestine and perhaps our own. In many ways, they still offer a non-conformist and counter-cultural view of being human to our own modern culture which in many respects is still just as brutish and inhumane as Rome was.

The next segment of the Sermon is the "salt and light" metaphor. Jesus tells his disciples they are to be the salt of the earth, a practical ingredient to all that sustains life. They are also to be the light, which implies hope for humanity. These are earthly, human themes that don't speak to how one gets to heaven and avoids hell, but how one reflects the salt and light of the inner life of faith to a world in need.

Perhaps the largest segment of the Sermon on the Mount is given to juxtaposing "what you have heard it said" with "here is a new way to act, think and reflect one's faith."

Jesus deals with basic human emotions and reactions such as anger, lust, revenge, and how to treat your enemies. Each teaching draws a line of comparison from an emphasis on the external law to the inner life. Each statement Jesus makes turns the individual inward to assess their own life and behavior by the inner consciousness of the heart.

Ultimately this segment ends with encouragement to care for the needs of the less fortunate and practicing one's outward faith in privacy and in secret. Religious ritual is to be more a matter of the heart than outward show.

Jesus then admonishes his followers not to pray like the showy priests in the Temple, or I suppose in today's culture, the television preachers. Prayer for Jesus is again an inward orientation of focus on the kingdom of God which is already present within each person. Prayer isn't a grandstanding event but a closed personal mediation and connective moment.

Toward the end of the Sermon Jesus begins to speak to basic human priorities and motivations. He speaks out against crass materialism as in laying up for yourselves treasures on earth as opposed to treasures in heaven.

Yes, there is the word finally, heaven. In this context, it is more about providing benefit to those around us as opposed to selfish hoarding of money. Jesus also warns against judging others and encourages followers not to be anxious.

The capstone of the sermon is the golden rule, which is a common theme in almost all world religious traditions. There is something so human and yet divine in doing something as simple as treating others the way we would want to be treated. If this were easy to do humanly speaking it wouldn't need to be a cornerstone of virtually every major religious tradition.

The highest call of being human and living a life worthy of this inner kingdom of God is in how we treat others. It's not what doctrinal statement I profess nor what theology I subscribe to. As Paul wrote, without Love, all preaching is a clanging cymbal and simply an annoying sound.

Nothing in the Sermon on the Mount was instructive of how to gain entry into heaven and to avoid hell. The whole monologue was about this life and how to call out the most human of qualities and characteristics such as love, mercy, compassion and kindness.

The 5th Century theologian Augustine said this about the Sermon on the Mount, "If anyone will piously and soberly consider the sermon which our Lord Jesus Christ spoke on the mount, as we read it in the Gospel according to Matthew, I think that he will find in it, so far as regards the highest morals, a perfect standard of the Christian life." I would only add any life, Christian life or any life.

Evangelicals seem overly worried about making America great again these days, which by implication means, "Make America Christian again." If that means applying the precepts and principles of the Sermon on the Mount to our national life, I am all for it. If that means making our country a peaceful force throughout the world, ending wanton materialism, feeding the poor without regret and extending love to all regardless of race, gender or religion, then yes, let's make America great.

But, if it means let's turn America into a "Constantinian" theocratic-dogmatic nation that forces people to abide by some new Christian law which strips people of freedom and dignity, then that will actually serve to destroy the Republic in which we live by ending freedom of thought and religion, then I want no part of such a fascist regime.

Jesus was a humanist, and I believe it is time to bring Christianity back to its roots and foundation, a Christo-Humanism.

TWENTY-ONE

THANKING DONALD TRUMP

Perhaps some individuals, when they look in the mirror held up by Trump, may not like what they see reflected back and decide that this is not really who or where they want to be, nor what they want their country to be. Such growth in personal awareness that leads to greater rather than less tolerance renders the fabric of our country that much stronger.[1]

—**Bob Madgic**, OpEd from 2016

ON NOV. 9, 2016, I was as stunned as anyone that Donald J. Trump had become the President of the United States in an unexpected, unpredicted, and unwelcome electoral victory. I remember a knot in the pit of my stomach that kept me up most of the night and watching late election returns only made it worse.

In the strangest irony that only history can produce and appreciate, what Trump has unleashed in this country is truly remarkable and in hindsight, I can be grateful that he has exposed the worst side of American culture and especially American Evangelical culture, for what it is. The anger, bigotry, hatred, racism, division, and hostility that has been unleashed is just now in 2020's, beginning to turn the tide of history in a way that I don't think Hillary Clinton could have done.

The irony of it is that many positive social movements and changes are now beginning to coalesce and take shape. Change of this magnitude can only be accomplished in reaction to an existential crisis moment in time. That is where we are.

Let me go back to 2016. I was in Milwaukee on business a few nights after the election, and setting in a pub in the downtown area, I was startled to look up to see a parade of people marching through the downtown area carrying signs and chanting anti-Trump slogans. It was young people, all races, and many, many women. This was well before the Women's March in January. From day one a sleeping giant had been awakened.

It was no secret what values Trump stood for, and this reaction which was visceral and immediate seemed to electrify thousands of people in a way that they might have never experienced before. They were making a statement that Donald Trump's values are not our values. We are not Donald Trump, and his America will not be our America. But the only problem was that a certain portion of America does reflect Donald Trump's values. To some degree we are Donald Trump.

But let me be clear about what it is I'm thanking Donald Trump for. It isn't for "Making America Great" because he hasn't accomplished that, and it isn't because he wanted to build a "great big, beautiful wall" to keep immigrants out.

What I think Trump has done and will probably be remembered for the most is this:

He has exposed the dark, ugly underbelly of American culture and held up a mirror to especially white Christian Americans and said, "see, take a look at yourself, this is what you are! You are greedy, you are bigoted, you are narcissistic, you are religious but only for political gain, you are sexist, you are anti-science, you are conspiratorialists, you are petty, you are vengeful, you are racists, and...you are just like me!"

Trump reflects what a large swath of the American people already are. He didn't create it; he reflected it back and projected it to enough people that envied him and saw themselves in him to squeak out an electoral victory. That is what stunned, shocked, and saddened so many of us.

For Evangelicals, their support and adoration for Donald Trump was a moment of truth. The masks came off and the pretense was gone. What Evangelicals have been morphing into for the past four decades was revealed in bold living color with the election of Trump and their 81% support for him. The thirst for political power, the both subtle and overt racism of the churches, the patriarchy of male-dominated institutions and the hatred and fear of the "other" in the form of immigrants was all revealed at once. Evangelicals came out of the closet, and said, "yes, that is us."

So, thank you Donald Trump. You have exposed the truth about what the Evangelical movement has become, and it is an ugly scene.

And for Evangelicals they no longer need to pretend to be spiritual or to care about others or even to proclaim the "good news" for all people. They can now publicly espouse their bigotry and hatred for the "least of these" that they have harbored all along but were too afraid to admit publicly.

Help the refugees? See to the needs of the poor? Care for the elderly, the widows and those in prison? No need to even pretend to do those things now. Donald Trump has given them permission to be as crass and unfeeling about their fellow human beings as he is.

It isn't new. Many saw this happening years ago and left. For others it is a more recent exodus since 2016.

Perhaps the most revealing part of what Trump has exposed is the racial bigotry that has been part and parcel of Christianity for centuries. Trump's slogan, "Make America Great Again" is code for "Make America White and Christian Again."

With declining demographic numbers, white Evangelicals are desperate to cling to the power and privilege that has been afforded them in earlier days when the white population was around 89%. Today the white population is just a nose above 60%, and if you take the under age 16 crowd white-young people are under 50% for the first time in history.[2]

White Christianity in the US is on the decline and hitching a wagon to the Trump train is a last bid effort to revive that dying demographic. It is estimated by 2045 whites as a group will make up less than 50% of the American population for the first time in the nation's history.[3]

That is why Evangelicals are so desperate to define what a "true American" is. Donald Trump has given Evangelicals permission to marginalize non-white populations, encourage white nationalism and promote racist immigration policies in order to protect a white Christian Ethno-State. Angry white evangelicals are getting louder and more aggressive in their speech as well as their actions. It was no coincidence that many of the signs being waved at the January 6th attack on the Capitol in Washington, contained Nationalistic Christian messages.

Unfortunately, for many decades as Americans took pride in becoming more progressive and socially tolerant, it was as if we felt asleep at the wheel, taking it for granted that we were on our way toward a bright future where racism, sexism and all the other social evils were non-existent.

At least that is what we told ourselves. After all, same sex marriage had become legal in all states, and we had a black President for the first time in the nation's history. Women, though still not paid on par with men, were making progress in education, science, and business. No one would have thought these were temporary gains or illusions.

But on November 9, 2016, the curtain was pulled back and Donald Trump laid bare the reality that our society was rotten at its core and the progress that we thought we had been making was token or perhaps illusory. It certainly is fragile.

Thus, the term "woke" was coined as the stunning realization that the mountain before us is steep and the progress we thought we had made was only in the foothills. Millions were awakened and found out that while being asleep at the wheel, we were careening completely off course and going over the cliff. This was existential in terms of who we are as a nation and where we were headed. The reaction now has been strong and swift.

There are four movements that are underway and coming together to create a moment in time ripe for social change. Again, these movements are awakening in part due to Donald Trump's worst inclinations as a leader and a person.

Women's Movement and "Me Too"

This movement was in motion as all of them were, prior to the ascendancy of Donald Trump. But as Americans looked in the mirror and saw what real misogyny looks like in the example of Trump and reflected that back to all of us, women have stood up like never before since the Suffrage movement of the early 20th Century.

Women and young people were especially at the forefront of this reaction. The Women's March on Jan. 21, the day after Trump's inauguration, was the first major salvo in this uprising. More than 3 million people marched the day after Trump's inauguration. Even in my small town in Iowa, we marched to protest not so much the policies of Trump but rather the values for which he stands with regard to women. A half a million people showed up in Washington D.C. alone.

The message was loud and clear.

"We aren't going to be treated this way anymore, and you cannot just grab women with impunity as you have boasted."

The protesters that took part in the various Women's March events voiced their support for various causes, including women's reproductive rights, criminal justice, defense of the environment and the rights of immigrants, Muslims, gay and transgender people and the disabled—all of whom were seen as particularly vulnerable under the new administration.

This event was not a one-time grand march. It has evolved into what came to be known as the "resistance." And, in the ensuing four years, it gained strength and followers.

Americans have rejected the reflection of Trump's mirror showing sexism, misogyny and disrespect for women and have concluded, "Let's break the mirror or at least change the image we see.

Young People and "March for Our Lives"

On February 14, 2018, a lone shooter entered Marjory Stoneman Douglas High School in Parkview, Florida and proceeded on a bloody rampage of shooting and killing. The toll was staggering. 17 students were killed, and hundreds were traumatized by the act of one active shooter with an AR 15.

Rather than act as victims, the students in the High School stood up and took action and within weeks had formed an organization and a march called "*March for Our Lives.*" This movement has been led by young people most of whom are not even old enough to vote. School walkouts were planned and the march on March 24 attracted over a million people who spoke out against needless gun violence, and the lack of federal law enforcement, policy, and action. On that day there were over 800 local events throughout the United States and internationally.

"*March for Our Lives*" is still an ongoing organization run mainly by young people. Their activism and work on behalf of common-sense gun reform is having an impact. This generation of young people are being raised on the diet of social activism and will eventually make a difference. Young people have seen the Trump mirror and have concluded that they want to change the image that they see.

"Black Lives Matter"

After 400 years of enslavement, segregation, Jim Crow laws, massacres, and other forms of systemic racism, it took one video of a policeman in Minneapolis to galvanize the whole nation, black and white, to react in an overwhelming show of force. The protests of course have been going on for decades since the days of the Civil Rights movement.

But this event in tandem with the racist comments and overtures by the Trump administration, has led to a moment when the majority of Americans have said, "*enough.*"

The injustice that was exposed in that video has led to efforts that include policing reform, but beyond that to demands for the removal of racist and offensive monuments and statues, changes in hiring practices that are discriminatory, and awareness of how housing redlining practices have harmed minority populations for decades. Change is in the air, and the "Black Lives Matter Movement" which was born several years ago, has gained new prominence as a social change agent.

Americans of all races and ethnic groups have peered into Trump's mirror and have concluded, that isn't who we are. We are better than that.

LGBTQ Rights

Despite the stacking of the Supreme Court with Justices hand-picked by conservative organizations like the "Federalist Society" , the court has chosen an independent path in regard to LGBTQ rights. It is apparent that the US will not go backwards on this issue since the Supreme Court decision in 2015 legalizing gay marriages.

The movement to truly realize the dream of equal rights for all has been again recognized by the Roberts court in a 6-3 decision in *"Bostock v. Clayton County, Ga.*" The decision forbids discrimination of people in the workplace on account of "sex" which the court has ruled includes gay and transgender people. This was a blow to the Trump administration who was using this case as a way to garner votes especially from the Evangelical community which is still overtly anti-gay. Americans have looked in the Trump mirror and have concluded, that is not who we are.

The reaction and movements across the country in the past four years have come swiftly and with the power that only local participation and involvement can motivate. Social change never comes in pacific waters. Only when there is cruelty, outrage, injustice, and mistreatment does culture react in such a determined way. It has happened only a few times in American history, but this current era will certainly go down as one of them.

A noticeable absence in these four movements are Evangelicals. This will be a historic opportunity missed for those that claim to follow the teachings of Jesus. Historically, Evangelicals have been involved in important social reform movements. If they would join forces with the leaders of these movements, an authentic faith impact could be useful in bringing about justice.

Once again what Donald Trump has revealed is that Evangelical Christianity isn't interested in fighting for women's rights and integrity, or standing up for black lives, or extending a loving hand to the LGBTQ community or assisting young people looking for positive ways to reduce gun violence.

We can thank Donald Trump for providing the fuel for the engine of change that is currently taking place. For me I see hope for change. I see women, young people, blacks and whites, young and old coming together to reject the image of Donald Trump that he has unleashed on the country.

The realization that the problem is us, and not just Donald Trump, is the real "woke" moment. We need to change ourselves and our culture. If we can do that people like Trump will take their mirrors and go home. Thank you Donald Trump.... for unleashing this moment of self-reflection and change that swept you out of office and will help to create a more just and caring society.

Twenty-Two

LABELS AND OTHER FORMS OF TRIBALISM

The toxic mix of religion and tribalism has become so dangerous as to justify taking seriously the alternative view, that humanism based on science is the effective antidote, the light and the way at last placed before us.[1]

—**E. O. Wilson,** Author

Growing up in a conservative-evangelical church, I saw the world in a binary way. There were "believers" and "non-believers," "Christians" and "Non-Christians" and there were those that were "born again" and those that were, for lack of a better term, "unregenerate." I was taught from a young age to classify people into two groups and use the labels to determine their character and what they "needed" spiritually.

Ultimately this led to an unmistakable and precise "Us vs. Them" mentality that immediately made some people friends and others suspects or targets for evangelism. It all made for a clearly defined and certain world to assess the people around me.

Using labels and tribal thinking is a quick and convenient way for humans to make decisions about other people. For every label or category that we have in our minds, we associate a set of beliefs or actions with that group. It is the classic straw man argument where we build up a mental picture of someone based on assumptions and generalities and immediately tear the straw man apart and dismiss them because we now associate them with the straw man. It is a lazy way to interact with people and it is demeaning.

The labels and consequent tribal identity didn't end with generalities such as "Christian" or "non-Christian." The labeling went much further into "*what kind of Christian are you?*"

So, are you the Calvinist kind of Christian, or the Arminian kind? Are you a Baptist Christian or a Catholic Christian? Are you a Premillennialist type of Christian or Post-Millennial type of Christian? All these labels allowed me to neatly categorize anyone I ran into and make broad generalizations about their beliefs, character and how I should interact with them, or not.

The label gave me a mental map or script and I was able to prejudge them before ever actually getting to know them as a human being. And that is the trap of labels and tribalism. It never allows us to view people as human beings first and above all else. We don't take the time to talk, ask questions, learn their history, and discover the nuanced story that makes each person unique, but also similar to us.

It isn't surprising that tribalism is rampant in religion. We see it everywhere: politics, sports, nations, and gangs within neighborhoods. Sometimes tribalism is good-natured fun as in cheering on your favorite sports team or school. But it can also be deadly as in gang violence and war between nations.

It is likely that this tendency toward tribal affinity is part of our genetic code that was ingrained thousands of years ago. It allowed early Sapiens to survive in a hostile world where one wrong move could mean death from a wild animal or competing group. Affinity with a tribe or group meant survival, belonging and protection.

Tribalism has allowed our species of humans to dominate the world and has led to the destruction of other species of humans, the decimation of eco-systems, the extinction of thousands of species of other plants and animals, and the genocide of other Sapiens who were of a different tribe. But that is how tribalism works isn't it? One group survives and the other one doesn't. One group is secure and the other one is decimated.

It isn't religion's fault if there is extreme tribal affinity even within a single religion, let alone between competing religions. There seems to be a biological need to identify with a group for safety and survivals sake. But when you add to the mixture of religious belief which is supernatural in nature, humans can justify just about any type of abuse, cruelty, genocide, and hatred to assure the survival and protection of their religious group. If God has decreed that your group is "chosen" or "special" or a "remnant" of some sort that has divine sanction and approval, then any action taken to ensure your safety and protection is approved by an all-powerful deity. Morality be damned.

We have seen this play out time and again in history, over and over. The Crusades, and the genocide of native tribes in South America and North America in the name of Christ are just a couple of examples. Humans are ingenious at finding justifications for imposing death on other humans while all the time claiming divine justification for their group. The Bible is full of such examples.

The Salem Witch trials are another good example of religious tribalism leading to death. I recently discovered through genealogical research, that my 9th great-grandmother, Margaret Scott, was hanged as a witch in 1692. She was part of one of the last groups of accused individuals that were not part of the Puritan tribe in an appropriate way and paid the ultimate price. My ninth great-grandmother was a widow and was in her 70's when she was accused of witchcraft. It is likely she was the oldest person executed during the witch trials in Salem. Because she was a widow and was left destitute when she reached old age, she was reduced to begging for basic necessities.

The Puritan mindset saw begging and poverty as disapproval from God, and they found her pleas for help most likely to be annoying and it created guilt in their consciences which they could not accept. She was outside of the main tribe of her village in Rowley, Massachusetts, when a more well-to-do family accused her of sickening their cow and casting spells on other members of their family. She was jailed, tried in a cursory way, and condemned to death by her neighbors. It wasn't until 2001 that the Massachusetts state legislature exonerated her and expressed remorse for the actions of civil authorities.[2]

Tribalism is not just a human oddity and vestige of human biology; it is deadly serious business. Millions of people have died from irrational human tribal connections. So, as I consider the role that tribalism has played in my own life during my years as a young Evangelical, I am reminded just how easy it was to view others outside of my tribe as less than acceptable, which is disturbingly close to "less than human."

Here is what I mean. Shortly after my conversion to Christ at the age of 12, I was told that I was now born-again and a follower of Christ and those that didn't have Christ as their savior were somehow lost and in danger of burning in hell for eternity.

Now that message puts me in a special class of people. I was in the "in-crowd" and accepted by an all-powerful deity that now threatened to annihilate all of those who weren't like me. Of course, I was obligated to spread the message of the "good news" about accepting Jesus as a personal savior so that others could be in the eternal in-group and avoid burning in hell.

I did my best, but what I remember is thinking about how "different" everyone else was that didn't have that born-again experience. They were not like me and somehow, I was in a class different from them, even though I was never taught to think that way, it was simply a natural outcome.

I mean if I was going to heaven and spending eternity in eternal bliss in the presence of God, and others were going to go to hell to be tortured for eternity because they weren't like me, well I guess I was a bit better, wasn't

I? God loved everyone, or so I was taught, but maybe he loved me a bit more than those unfortunate eternally damned friends of mine.

Here is the practical application of this tribal mentality. As a teenager, I deliberately separated myself from my "unsaved" friends in school. I backed out of having contact with too many of my peers that were not of the same tribe as I. Eventually I dropped out of sports, baseball, and other common activities. I dropped out of music programs to spend more time with my peers in the church youth group.

Some conservative churches required "separation" from others not of their denomination or affiliation. My church didn't require it, but it seemed like a natural course of action to reduce contact with those that were going to hell and spend more time with those that were like me, the blessed and eternally destined crew.

For many years I would only associate with others from my church and youth group. If we ventured into "unsaved" territory it was only to proselytize the lost and bring them into the fold of the saved and favored. The arrogance and condescension were palpable. We reeked of hubris. But why not? We were the chosen.

But here is the funny thing that I discovered. The chosen group that I decided to associate with was no different than the unchosen that I left behind. And neither was I. I was walking around with the naïve notion that my peers in the Jesus group were somehow morally more upright and nicer than the non-believers and qualitatively more righteous. It wasn't true. Over time I found out that my crew mates were no different than anyone else. They could be just as mean, petty, disloyal, vindictive, and cruel as anyone else. And that included me.

I had high expectations for our behavior and attitudes but in the end, we were all the same...we were just humans. Our claims to righteousness did nothing to improve our character, and in fact, it made us worse characters in many respects because of the pride.

Our denominational statement of beliefs and creeds did nothing to improve our behavior and our prayers had little effect as well. Being "filled with the Holy Spirit" was meant to create some sort of sanctification work within our lives; but it only gave a momentary religious ecstasy or feeling and more reason to feel superior to everyone else. There was no transformation of the soul leading to better dispositions toward fellow humans.

Reflecting on my own church experience over several decades has led me to conclude that most church environments are toxic and do damage to those that stay in them. Whether it is a church fight leading to split, gossip about others down the pew from us, and the affairs and sexual abuses that are now well documented, being in a church can be a disgraceful and depressing experience.

And of course, there was always the pressure to present a veneer of religious conversation, imagery, and personality. It was like having to behave in ways that made you less human while you were at church, ways that you didn't express anywhere else during the week. It was stressful having to leave my humanity at the door.

Leaving the church was a liberating experience and leaving behind all notions of the binary nature of people has also opened me to new experiences, and new spiritual development.

It seems funny to say this, although not surprising, but I had to get away from the church environment to discover God in new and refreshing ways. The church environment was simply too unhealthy psychologically and spiritually.

That is the point, isn't it? In taking a more nuanced look at Jesus' life and teachings, I am of the opinion now that 95% of what goes on in churches has little to do with what Jesus was teaching his followers. In fact, it may just be the opposite. Jesus never said make a creed out of your interpretations of my teachings and require everyone to accept them. Jesus never said let's start a new religion and set up a religious empire. Jesus never even said that people ought to worship him. That all came later.

What has emerged over the centuries in the development of Christianity is a religious system that is just as captive to tribalism as any other religious system ever devised. And I'm not sure Jesus had any desire to see his followers become tribal, exclusive, or binary. And it didn't take long for that to happen, did it? In 1 Corinthians 1, Paul says:

> . . . it has been reported to me by Chloe's people that there are quarrels among you, my brothers and sisters. What I mean is that each of you says, "I belong to Paul," or "I belong to Apollos," or "I belong to Cephas," or "I belong to Christ." Has Christ been divided?

Tribalism is a difficult tendency to oppose within the human heart. But I'm beginning to think that this was the very essence of what Jesus was trying to teach us. Perhaps he was trying to show us how to overcome our own personal tribalism. Perhaps the most important and transformative thing that Jesus taught, modeled, and tried to get his followers to see is that we should overcome the biological or evolutionary need to be tribal.

Think about all the things that Jesus said or did that contradict the human need for separation and tribal affinity:

Jesus washed the feet of his disciples, a role reversal of typical rabbinical leaders,

Jesus associated with Samaritans who were not friendly to Jews and deliberately challenged tribal boundaries,

Jesus taught his followers to be one with God, and with each other, everyone!

Jesus criticized the religious leaders of his day who had separated themselves into superior groups and put obstacles in the way of other people searching for God,

Jesus allowed women to be part of his entourage and spoke to them as equals,

Jesus blessed the traitorous tax collector Zacchaeus, who was an outcast in his own Jewish tribe,

Jesus always associated with the marginalized and disgraced people of his society, he never grouped them or his followers into a new tribe,

Everything that Jesus taught was about breaking down barriers, boundaries and tribes and viewing all people as one,

Ultimately, Jesus taught that the Kingdom of God is within us. It isn't out there in a political entity or religion and certainly not in any new religion he was starting.

The universality of connection between all human beings and God (however you may want to define that term) is the ultimate tribal breaker. Another way to put it is, the only tribe we need to consider ourselves a member of is, the human race. Our sense of belonging and security can only be fulfilled in becoming fully and totally human...period. That is where God's kingdom thrives.

I'll admit this is a hard one for me as it probably is for everyone. Think of what it takes to interact and approach people without any reference to their so-called tribe: no religious tribe, no political tribe, no racial distinction, no gender distinction, just simply approach people as humans.

This will take some hard work to overcome the automatic categories that arise in my mind if I meet someone for the first time and they have different skin color, or accent, or ethnicity. Perhaps they wear different religious garb that identifies their tribe. I think it will take some time to train my own mind to not prejudge or make any conclusions about the person until I've talked to them, listen to them, and understand the common humanity that we share between us.

But that is the hard part...talking to understand...listening without interrupting...and looking for our commonalities not superficial differences. Following Jesus is a hard thing not because we need to define our group, religion, denomination, or tribe, but because everything he taught runs counter to the need for those tribal affiliations.

TWENTY-THREE

BACK TO THE BEGINNING

CHANGING HOW I TEACH HISTORY

One of the saddest lessons of history is this: If we've been bamboozled long enough, we tend to reject any evidence of the bamboozle. We're no longer interested in finding out the truth. The bamboozle has captured us. It's simply too painful to acknowledge, even to ourselves, that we've been taken. Once you give a charlatan power over you, you almost never get it back.[1]

—**Carl Sagan**, *The Demon Haunted World*

EARLY IN MY TEACHING career my goal and purpose were to teach students history from a "Christian World and Life View." What that meant was every event, time-period, epoch, or era was to be filtered through the lens of the Bible and a white Protestant American interpretation of those events.

What it meant specifically is that God is in control of all world events and Christians and the Church were to be the focus and center of history. America was to be considered God's new Israel in the modern age and special blessings would pour down on the nation if they remained true to God.

Individuals that did great things were generally considered to be doing God's will and evil people were evidence of Satan's work in our world.

It also meant that history had a definitive beginning with the creation of the world as taught in Genesis and will have an ultimate conclusion with the return of Christ to create a New Heaven and New Earth as taught in the book of Revelation. These two books, *Genesis* and *Revelation* are bookends to all of history.

Mostly what was required was to indoctrinate students that the United States was a Christian nation. On this point there could be no equivocation. The textbooks that were used came from Bob Jones University or other Christian Colleges and Seminaries. All the materials we used were unanimous on this point. To suggest that the founders of the country were anything other than white Protestant committed Christians was to invite the wrath of the school board down on your head in a private Evangelical religious school.

I was never fully comfortable with this singular point of view regarding the founding of the United States. I still, even in my most Christian Nationalistic days, found a way to bring other elements to the discussion such as the Enlightenment. And I couldn't ignore the fact that some of the founders were Deists and in some cases atheists. As a historian I simply couldn't in all honesty ignore these obvious historical truths. But these were cursory discussions.

The most popular books recommended to students were works such as Peter Marshall's "*The Light and The Glory*" that explains in detail the special plan that God has for the United States.

Added to this mix was David Barton's Christian Nationalistic writings many of which have been criticized by even other Evangelicals for loose quotations and misrepresentations. The point is these writings provided a steady diet of flag waving, Bible-thumping, privilege making lessons that indoctrinated a generation of young people in Christian Patriotism who are now coming of age.

But what my colleagues and I were doing was teaching a form of Christian Nationalism that now threatens the foundations of the Democratic-Republic that is the United States.

We taught the idea that the separation of church and state was a one-way street as David Barton argues. The government couldn't interfere in religion or establish a state church, but the Christian religion was considered the "unofficial" state religion by virtue of God's grace and the *Declaration of Independence*. The ultimate outcome of such an idea is a theocratic republic with Christians having primary control of the levers of power and Christianity given preferential status in society while giving token tolerance to other religions.

Here is the problem with this line of teaching. Young people actually believed it! And now that they are the generation inheriting leadership roles in government, business, and educational institutions it is no wonder there are movements afoot to install "Christian values" at all levels of society despite the shrinking demographic that Christians represent. Having been involved and partially responsible for teaching young people many of these false ideas my goal has become to undo and reverse as much of this atrocity as possible.

What is most troubling about the students that I taught in the 1980s and 90s. Many of them (thank goodness, not all) have become staunch Donald Trump supporters while at the same time espousing Evangelical Christianity. They seem to be in good company since around 81% of evangelicals have supported Trump in both the 2016 and 2020 elections.[2]

Somewhere between the 1980's and 2016 the idea that "America is a Christian Nation" merged with "Make America Great Again" and that emerged in the form of a populist nationalist movement spurred on by Donald Trump. It is better described as having been manipulated by Trump.

Gone was any pretense of religious ethics or morality. The Evangelicals that I taught two decades ago now promoted a man whose character was so flawed that he never even admitted to needing anyone's forgiveness, not even God's.

In the 1990's Evangelicals excoriated Bill Clinton for his character failures but by 2016, adultery, sexual predatory behavior and outward expressions of sexual exploitation were no longer disqualifying to the Evangelical community.

I heard and read rationalizations from former students trying to justify their support for Trump. The justifications ranged from the "Cyrus argument," the one where in the Old Testament God uses a heathen king to free the nation of Israel so they can return to their homeland, to a more cynical argument that "we aren't electing a pastor, but a President." In either case, Christian morality and ethics flew out the door as fast as a MAGA hat being thrown out at a Trump rally.

What is particularly disheartening about this convergence is to see many former students that I've known over the years express policy positions that run directly opposite of Jesus' teachings. Build the wall and close the borders instead of welcoming the stranger and taking care of refugees. Line the pockets of wealthy people in society with unnecessary tax cuts is now somehow a "Christian" message, Praise the Lord. And perhaps most insidious of all are the cries I hear calling out "All Lives Matter" when someone mentions "Black Lives Matter." It is a cruel and heartless retort that continues the marginalization of people of color in our society.

Jesus' teachings to weep with those that weep, grieve with those that grieve, and to extend mercy and love are somehow drowned out by a Christian Nationalistic chant to *Make America Great*, which is comingled with *Make America Christian* again.

The year 2016 was certainly a turning point in American history, but it was particularly grieving to me to see people that I know and love throw their support to the Trump movement and cloak it in a religious disguise. Evangelicals have sold their religious souls to the illusion of a secular savior who no more cares about their interests than he does his marriage vows to his several wives. He only cares about them so long as they support, adore, praise him, and give money to him.

The Evangelical movement is bankrupt and has abdicated any role in society to be a conscience to the powerful or prophetic voice to restrain evil and call out abuses of the poor and marginalized. And my role in this trajectory is a grievous mistake for which I feel compelled to pay penance and attempt to do what I can to perhaps undo or lessen the impact.

Going forward I have made it my mission to continue to teach history but in a way that will highlight truth instead of indoctrination, evidence instead of ideology and accuracy instead of propaganda. This is a tall order, and it isn't my objective here to produce a full philosophy of history. However, it is key to identify an approach to history that will provide guardrails and checks and balances to this endeavor.

So, what is the new approach? I'll summarize a few of the guardrails that I think are important.

Humility: The guardrails themselves need to be grounded in the attitude of humility. In my early career, teaching history was a matter of telling students what to believe from a position of pseudo-authority. The authority being the Bible. In this regard any deviation or challenge to the historical narrative was not encouraged or allowed.

Teaching like this was arrogant and unquestioned. The purpose was memorization and recitation. Here are the "facts" and your job as a student is to parrot those facts back to me. Those that parrot them the best get the highest grades.

Humility in teaching history is fundamental. The topic is so challenging and broad that anything less than humility will make it an exercise in arrogance. But to teach history from the foundation of humility means that questioning, doubting and challenging are not only encouraged, *they become the goal*.

As an instructor my role isn't to dispense historical knowledge in an authoritarian manner that goes unquestioned but to facilitate historical inquiry and elicit challenges to all suppositions and premises.

Another way to say it is that just because a teacher says it, doesn't make it so. And a teacher of history will need to have an attitude of humility to engage in debate and discussion of alternate viewpoints. It starts by admitting that my own perspective could be wrong and subject to unconscious or even conscious bias. Teaching as a process needs to be divorced from personal ego.

The other guardrails that I have committed to include:

Honesty: history has been used too often to promote a distorted view of the past to create a new reality about the present, or future. Using history in this way distorts and provides a dishonest view of past events. This seems to be the purpose behind the current raft of legislation, mainly in red states, that promote "patriotic history" and "Americanism."

History that is designed to promote patriotism (as some define it) or Americanism will include a white-washed view of people and events. Any time you see the word "patriotic" in front of the word history, you can bet it will be propaganda. It will attempt to hide or obfuscate events that contradict the narrative.

So, for example, in "patriotic history" the horror of the slave trade will be given little or no emphasis in the story of the United States. By leaving this out or reducing its importance, the history lesson is propagating a lie through distortion. Providing an honest and balanced account of people and events may not always make people feel good but it does promote the truth.

A popular saying that many people overuse is, "history is written by the victors." Many times, this has been true, and history has been used to justify or sanctify various actions taken by the victor to sanitize their reputations.

An example here is the conventional story surrounding the use of the atomic bomb in World War II. The "victors" have tried to justify this action through various interpretations of what Japan was or wasn't doing to bring the war to a close. The conclusion is that President Truman was justified in using such a weapon to save American lives.

Was he?

Recent scholarship has brought this traditional interpretation into question. There is evidence to suggest that Japan may have capitulated anyway regardless of the use of an atomic weapon. This will not make many Americans feel good; but it may be a more honest narrative.

But it isn't just the victors that get to tell the story in a slanted and distorted version. After the American Civil War southerners attempted to sanitize their efforts and reduce the stigma of slavery as a cause for the war. They rewrote the Civil War narrative in what came to be known as the "Lost Cause" southern narrative.

In this narrative, slavery really wasn't the primary cause of the Civil War, but northern encroachment on the culture and society of the agrarian south was the primary trigger. The average Confederate soldier was fighting to defend their property and way of life and it was a noble cause. It is the same justification for raising statues of Confederate generals and Confederate battle flags over statehouses. The south may have lost the war, but they may have won the propaganda battle that has been waging on ever since.

Accuracy: to teach history in an honest fashion it needs to be accurate. In other words, history should be evidence based, set within its context, and verified by multiple sources when possible. This is how history works.

Doing history this way is so much more difficult than teaching history for patriotic or nationalistic reasons. It is much easier to paint a false narrative on scant evidence to promote concepts that only exist in the mind. Watch a first-grade Thanksgiving pageant and you will see what I mean.

First, students need to learn how to analyze and interrogate historical sources. A textbook is not a historical source unless that textbook was perhaps written at the time in history under study.

Students should be able to distinguish between primary and secondary sources and then learn to ask deep and probing questions about both. What are the biases of the historical sources? Who wrote them and why might they want to present a particular event in a certain way? Do they have something to gain from this narrative? How accurate is the account of the event?

A good example is the Bible itself. Without a doubt there is important historical information to be gleaned from the narratives, but if students were taught to interrogate the sources and seek out motivations and biases of the writers, they may come to a much more balanced view of the Bible itself. Unfortunately, Evangelicals tend to see such reasoned interrogation as an attack and a risk to Biblical inerrancy.

Next, students need to understand the historical context of any event or time period. What this simply means is the ability to understand the culture of that time, the religion and beliefs of that group or individual, the level of scientific understanding or lack thereof. What were the values and beliefs of that group of people in that age? How did the culture impact their actions and decisions? Did their cultural blueprint justify their actions and decisions or were there some types of universal human ethos that could have played into their actions?

A key discussion around context can be applied to the south during ante-bellum slavery. To what degree can you absolve slaveholders because of the culture they created, or the common beliefs held? Can we use modern standards and values to evaluate the actions of slaveholding southerners? Is it fair or unfair to do so? You can see immediately this is a much more nuanced and deeper discussion than what "patriotic history" would allow.

Using multiple sources is an extension of evidence-based history and context. The more sources available the more layered and complex the discussion can become around various events. Which sources are better than others? Which came first? What other sources are missing?

A wonderful application of this element of historical study is the Bible. Once students begin to critically analyze the Bible as a primary source and compare it to other sources of the same time-period, a whole new vista of understanding can open.

Simply consider the four synoptic gospels for instance. Which of these sources was written first? To what degree do these accounts represent first-hand narratives? Do any of the gospels rely on any others for their information? Do any of the gospels rely on outside or other unknown sources of information? How long after the events they describe were they written? This type of interrogation can go on *ad infinitum*. Again, the Evangelical straight jacket would certainly discourage such an approach.

Agenda Free: this follows from teaching history in an *honest* way and being *accurate.* Before studying history in an evidence-based and accurate way, one will need to check at the door their own implicit biases if they know what they are. Leave behind any attempt to use history to verify a religious point of view or to create patriotic feelings of nationalism.

For many years I was encouraged to use history to prove the efficacy and credibility of the Bible. And I was encouraged to use history to create God-loving, flag-waving patriots that believed that the United States was a "special nation" blessed by God with a special mission. In a word it was indoctrination or at worse it was brainwashing. It was dishonest and it was inaccurate.

Ultimately an agenda-free approach to history will require students to engage in the most human of all conscious endeavors: critical thinking. The approaches I've described are nothing more than critical thinking applied to historical study. Teaching history is as much about teaching critical thinking as it is events, dates, trends, or people. And I might add, way more exciting.

One approach that I have used in the latter part of my teaching career is designed to promote just such critical analysis. I call it...

The Four-Corners Approach: in this type of history lesson, I use the analogy of a traffic accident happening at an intersection with four corners. There is a bystander on each corner, and they all witness the accident. Each person on each corner files a report when the police arrive to investigate but each is different in their telling of events and in their blame for who is responsible. Each corner provides a different perspective or angle from which the witness saw what happened. They were all first-hand witnesses but why were their accounts and reports so different? Was it the angle or shadow from their corner that shaded or colored what happened? What were their age's and how good was their eyesight? What were their occupations and how did that influence their report?

Applying this framework to the American Revolution let's say we have four different people that witnessed the "Boston Massacre" on March 5, 1770. On one corner there was a fiery revolutionary by the name of Samuel Adams. On another corner was a British customs agent that had been harassed by colonials. On another corner was a Frenchman who was visiting relatives in Boston that year. And finally, on the fourth corner was a free black man who is subject to discrimination. Students would be asked to think from the perspective of each of these witnesses and analyze or create an account of what happened.

The facts are not in dispute: someone shot first, several people were killed, and British troops were involved. What was going on prior to the shooting? Why did someone fire? Who fired first? Were there other projectiles flying through the air to threaten the authorities? Who is to blame? Should the British soldiers be charged with murder? Should colonials be charged with assault?

It goes without saying this exercise leads to some provocative and challenging discussions, debate and conclusions. In fact, it is likely a student's understanding of the Boston Massacre changes depending on what corner they are standing on at the time.

And the goal isn't to prove which corner was right, but it is more to use critical thinking skills to see from another's perspective, look at one's own implicit biases and how they affect what you see, and to gain a deeper understanding of the event within its context of that time.

Hopefully students learn that the Boston Massacre was much more complex than simply colonials being shot down by British troops which made for great propaganda but was short on truth. There is way more to the story.

That is how I hope students will learn history. Yes, it requires that you abandon the good guys vs. bad guys categories and search for a much deeper analysis and understanding. It requires critical thought and application of historiography to the events. But the result I think will be young people that are much better prepared to engage in civic life within a multicultural and multi-religious community that the United States is becoming.

I repent of not having taught students early in my career in this manner. It would be easy for me to simply dismiss my own shortcomings as ignorance and speculate that they will probably all do just fine regardless. But I hope that through their forgiveness, forbearance and understanding I can help repair the damage or at least, provide a better way for their children and grandchildren to learn about history. And learn about themselves.

Twenty-Four

EPILOGUE

I HOPE YOU HAVE enjoyed this trip through my mind and my heart. The span of time that these discussions entail is quite vast starting in the 1950's to the present. For those that have known me over the years these chapters may be familiar and unremarkable. But for those that are former students and friends that I have not had contact with for many years, this story may come as a shock. Some will be surprised and even angry and some will be delighted. Either is ok. In the end I was writing as much for myself as I was for anyone else.

But I do hope that if nothing else my story will cause many to think, question, study, search, anguish, forgive and evolve in faith. You see I believe the concept of God is so much bigger and vast in scope than a narrow Evangelical mindset has ever perceived. It is bigger than I can ever perceive, define, or understand. That is why you and I need to keep on pursuing it.

The truth is I am still evolving and changing. I suspect that in a few short years I may come to question everything I've written here. And that is how it should be. Thomas Merton once said that "*if the me of five years ago doesn't see the me of today as a heretic, then I'm not growing or learning.*" I think that is true.

Change is the essence of learning. True learning...not parroting back doctrine and dogma, will always result in changing perspectives and understandings. If I seek truth and meaning and connections, then I will change, most certainly I will constantly change.

A few years ago, I had an online exchange with a former student of mine that was quite put out that I had changed my teaching and perspective on all things Evangelical and conservative. He asked me outright, "did you lie to us?" I saw right away that his "faith" was dependent on the supposed authority of other people...including me. That was a heartbreaking moment to me. I realized that I had unintentionally stolen the soul-searching capability of that student and replaced it with an authoritarian dictum that had no credibility other than my own finite human fallibility.

I was humbled and saddened. I apologized and told the young man that I was sorry, but I had no authority or governance over his soul. I ended the conversation by saying that his faith was his own to find and define...if he could. It wasn't dependent on me.

This is the penance I must pay. I have led too many young people astray in the pursuit of their own faith and truth. Certainty, finality, and absolutism gives a false sense of security that provides a level of laziness that allows for each person to rest on the authority of the "teacher' they trust.

The truth is their heart is their own teacher. They have the truth already resident inside of themselves. They need only to learn how to connect to and follow the truth within them.

Finally, let me say that despite my misgivings and concerns about the Evangelical movement in the United States, I am hopeful. Though our current time is filled with strife and angst and division, I believe we are headed in the right direction. Fundamentalist religious viewpoints are falling farther and farther out of the mainstream in every religion and culture. Our differences are being exploited by a salivating media and political and religious opportunists that only seek temporary advance power or ratings. These politico-religious Pharisees cannot sustain human development.

But as humans individually seek to become better humans, more humane and more humanistic, and leave the religious straightjackets behind, I think we are headed to a place where we begin to see each individual as Jesus did. As a friend, brother, sister, equal and fellow disciple. To that end Godspeed on your journey. You can take Christopher Dawson's thoughts with you as you go:

> Humanism and Divinity are as complementary to one another in the order of culture, as are Nature and Grace in the order of being.[1]
>
> —**Christopher Dawson**, English Historian

END NOTES

Introduction

1. Palmer, Jim. "Untangling the 'God Relationship' Problem." Jim Palmer, Author Blog. (December 1, 2021).
https://www.jimpalmerauthor.com/post/2018/11/10/untangling-the-god-relationship-problem.

2. Peck, Scott. *The Different Drum: Community Making and Peace*. New York: Touchstone, 1987, 190–93.

3. Merton, Thomas. *Contemplative Prayer*. New York: Image, 2009, 123.

Chapter 1

1. Trippet, Krista. *Becoming Wise: An Inquiry into the Mystery and Art of Living*. Penguin: Westmin_ster, 2016, 36.

2. Smith, Gregory. "About Three-in-Ten U.S. Adults Are Now Religiously Unaffiliated" *Pew Research Center*. (December 14, 2021).
https://www.pewresearch.org/religion/2021/12/14/about-three-in-ten-u-s-adults-are-now-religiousl y-unaffiliated/.

Chapter 2

1. Merton, Thomas. *No Man Is An Island.* Mariner Books, Boston, 2002, 42.

Chapter 5

1. Spong, John Shelby. *Biblical Literalism: A Gentile Heresy: A Journey Into a New Christianity Through the Doorway of Matthew's Gospel.* Harper One: San Francisco, 2016, 6.

Chapter 6

1. Spong, John Shelby, interview by Candace Chellew-Hodge, *Religious Dispatches*. (February 24, 2016).
https://religiondispatches.org/why-it-is-heresy-to-read-the-bible-literally-an-interview-with-john-shelby-spong/.

2. Rohr, Richard. "Interview with Richard Rohr: The (Biblical) Universal Christ" Interview by Pete Enns, *The Bible for Normal People*, audio 6:03, updated July 13, 2020. https://peteenns.com/a-contemplative-look-at-the-bible-with-richard-rohr/.

Chapter 7

1. Ibram Kendi, "How Racism Has Evolved Over The Last 2 U.S. Presidencies" Interview by Rachel Martin, *Morning Edition, NPR*. (August 14, 2019).
https://www.npr.org/2019/08/14/751027770/how-racism-has-evolved-over-the-last-2-u-s-presidencies.

2. Newport, Frank, "Black and White Attitudes Toward Police," *Gallup Review*. (August 2014).
https://news.gallup.com/poll/175088/gallup-review-black-white-attitudes-toward-police.aspx.

3. Robert Brame, "Study: Half of black males, 40 percent of white males arrested by age 23," *Journal of Crime and Delinquency*. (January 6, 2014).
https://phys.org/news/2014-01-black-males-percent-white-age.html.

4. Butler, Athena. *White Evangelical Racism: The Politics of Morality in America*. University of North Carolina Press, Chapel Hill, 2021, 176.

5. Ibid.

Chapter 8

1. Wise, Tim. "Why Juneteenth Matters for White People, Too." Yes Magazine. (June 18, 2021). https://www.yesmagazine.org/opinion/2021/06/18/juneteenth-white-people.

Chapter 9

1. Chavers, Linda. "What too many white people still don't understand about racism." *Boston Globe*. (June 9, 2020).
https://www.bostonglobe.com/2020/06/09/magazine/what-too-many-white-people-still-dont-understand-about-racism/.

Chapter 10

1. Graham, Billy. "Answers." The Billy Graham Evangelistic Association. (July 27, 2005).
https://billygraham.org/answer/do-you-think-our-nation-will-ever-completely-overcome-its-racism/.

2. Puett, Tiffany. "Protestantism's troubling history with white supremacy in the US." *The Conversation*. (July 10, 2022).
https://theconversation.com/protestantisms-troubling-history-with-white-supremacy-in-the-us-141438.

3. "Partisan Polarization Dominates Trump Era: Findings from the 2018 American Values Survey." Survey by *Public Religion Survey Institute*. 2018.
https://www.prri.org/research/partisan-polarization-dominates-trump-era-findings-from-the-2018-american-values-survey/.

4. Ibid.

Chapter 11

1. "Analysis: The Texas GOP, in Its Own Words." *East Texas Tribune*. (May 15, 2016).

https://www.texastribune.org/2016/05/15/analysis-texas-republicans-their-own-words/.

2. "Estimate of How Often LGBTQ Youth Attempted Suicide in the U.S." *The Trevor Project*. (March 11, 2021).

https://www.thetrevorproject.org/research-briefs/estimate-of-how-often-lgbtq-youth-attempt-suicid e-in-the-u-s/.

Chapter 13

1. "2019 National Human Trafficking Hotline Statistics." Polaris Project. (Accessed July, 2022).

https://polarisproject.org/2019-us-national-human-trafficking-hotline-statistics/.

2. "On gun violence, the United States is an outlier." *Institute for Health Metrics and Evaluation (IHME)*. (May 31, 2022).

https://www.healthdata.org/acting-data/gun-violence-united-states-outlier.

3. "Income, Poverty and Health Insurance Coverage in the United States: 2020." *United State Census Bureau*. (Sept. 14, 2021).

https://www.census.gov/newsroom/press-releases/2021/income-poverty-health-insurance-cover_ age.html.

4. "Correctional Populations in the United States, 2020 – Statistical Tables." *Bureau of Justice Statistics*. (Accessed July, 2022).

https://bjs.ojp.gov/library/publications/correctional-populations-united-states-2020-statistical-table s.

Chapter 14

1. Myers, Seth. "Why Straight Women Are Attracted to Gay Men." *Psychology Today*. (July 6, 2012).
https://www.psychologytoday.com/us/blog/insight-is-2020/201207/why-straight-women-are-at_
tracted-gay-men.

2. Ibid.

3. "Every 68 seconds, an American is sexually assaulted." *Rape, Abuse and Incest National Network*. (Accessed July 2022).
https://www.rainn.org/statistics.

4. Myers, Seth. "Why Straight Women Are Attracted to Gay Men." *Psychology Today*. (July 6, 2012).
https://www.psychologytoday.com/us/blog/insight-is-2020/201207/why-straight-women-are-at_
tracted-gay-men.

5. Ibid.

Chapter 15

1. Ingersoll, Julie J. Building God's Kingdom: Inside the World of Christian Reconstructionism. Oxford: Oxford University Press, 2015, 240–41.

2. Barton, David. *America's Godly Heritage*, DVD, 1995.

Chapter 16

1. Huelle, Troy, interview by email to the author, June 22, 2021.

2. Knepper, Marty, and Lawrence, John. The Book of Iowa Films. Berkeley: Book of Iowa Films Press, 2014, 78.

3. "Mike Pence at AIPAC Policy Conference." Vimeo, 2009.
https://vimeo.com/26637142.

4. Wong, Edward. "The Rapture and the Real World: Mike Pompeo Blends Beliefs and Policy." New York Times. (March 30, 2019).
https://www.nytimes.com/2019/03/30/us/politics/pompeo-christian-policy.html.

5. "Attorney General William P. Barr Delivers Remarks to the Law School and the De Nicola Center for Ethics and Culture at the University of Notre Dame." *The United States Department of Justice.* (October 21, 2019).
https://www.justice.gov/opa/speech/attorney-general-william-p-barr-delivers-remarks-law-school-and-de-nicola-center-ethics.

6. Mencimer, Stephanie. "Evangelicals Love Donald Trump for Many Reasons, But One of Them Is Especially Terrifying – End Times" *Mother Jones.* (January 23, 2020).
https://www.motherjones.com/politics/2020/01/evangelicals-are-anticipating-the-end-of-the-world-and-trump-is-listening/.

Chapter 17

1. Young, Shawn David. *Gray Sabbath: Jesus People USA, Evangelical Left, and the Evolution of Christian Rock*, New York: Columbia University Press, 2015, 31.

2. "Events: Election of Jimmy Carter Timeline," Quality Data on Religion by *Association of Religion Data Archives.* (Accessed July 2022).
https://www.thearda.com/timeline/events/event_44.asp.

Chapter 18

1. Du Mez, Kristin Kobes. *Jesus and John Wayne: How White Evangelicals Corrupted a Faith and Fractured a Nation.* New York: Liveright, 2020, 135.

2. Wikipedia. "This Present Darkness." *Wikipedia, The Free Encyclopedia.* (Accessed July 5, 2022).
https://en.wikipedia.org/w/index.php?title=This_Present_Darkness&oldid=1095157970.

3. Cox, Dustin. "The Cultural Impact of the Doctrine of 'Territorial Spirits.'" The Book Times. (November 24, 2020).
https://baos.pub/the-cultural-impact-of-the-doctrine-of-territorial-spirits-f5bbf04600e5.

4. Du Mez, *Jesus and John Wayne*, 176.

5. Ibid., 52.

6. Culver, Jordan. "'God, Guns and Freedom': A rural Alabama Ford dealership's Fourth of July promotion is a viral sensation," *USA Today.* (June 25, 2019).

https://onlinestore.usatoday.com/06252019-issue-of-usa-today-p19516.aspx.

7. Speare-Cole, Rebecca. "GOP Lt. Gov. Drives Around With Gun and Bible To Protest COVID Restrictions in Idaho as Cases Soar." *Newsweek*. (October 30, 2020).

https://www.newsweek.com/idaho-protest-coronavirus-video-lt-gov-gun-bible-1543499.

8. Ree, Joseph; Tahman, Bradley; Ross, Brian. "U.S. Military Weapons Inscribed with Secret 'Jesus' Bible Codes." ABC News Online. (January 15, 2010).

https://abcnews.go.com/Blotter/us-military-weapons-inscribed-secret-jesus-bible-codes/story?id=9575794.

9. Merritt, Jonathan. "Jerry Falwell Jr.'s Troubling Remarks on Guns." *The Atlantic*. (Dec. 6, 2016).

https://www.theatlantic.com/politics/archive/2015/12/jerry-falwell-jrs-troubling-remarks-on-guns/419019/.

10. "Which Religions Support Gun Control in the U.S.?" *Religion News Service*. (August 29, 2019).

https://religionnews.com/2019/08/29/which-religions-support-gun-control-in-the-us/.

11. "Does Jesus Want You to Own A Gun?" *Salina Journal*. (Sept. 18, 2021).

https://www.salina.com/story/lifestyle/faith/2020/09/18/does-jesus-want-you-to-own-gun/114894146/.

12. Ibid.

13. Ibid.

14. Joyce, Kathryn. "How Christian Nationalism Drove the Insurrection: A Religious History of Jan. 6." Salon. (January 6, 2022).

https://www.salon.com/2022/01/06/how-christian-nationalism-drove-the-insurrection-a-religious-history-of-jan-6/.

15. Copulsky, Jerome. "Introduction: A Religious, Yet Religiously Incoherent Event." *Uncivil Religion*. (January 6, 2021).

https://uncivilreligion.org/home/introduction.

Chapter 19

1. Chittister, Sister Joan. From an Interview with Bill Moyers, 2004.

https://vimeo.com/214085997.

2. Staff Report, House Judiciary Subcommittee on Civil & Constitutional Rights, 1993, with updates

by DPIC in 1995.

https://www.ojp.gov/pdffiles1/Photocopy/154463NCJRS.pdf.

3. Center for Disease Control. "Fast Facts: Firearm Violence Prevention."

https://www.cdc.gov/violenceprevention/firearms/fastfact.html.

4. Ibid.

5. Ibid.

6. Food Research and Action Center. "Community Eligibility: The Key to Hunger-Free Schools, Year 2021–2022."

https://frac.org.cep-report-2022.

7. "U.S. Defense Spending Compared to other Countries." *Peter G. Peterson Foundation*. (May 11, 2022).

https://www.pgpf.org/chart-archive/0053_defense-comparison.

8. OECD (2021). "Education at a Glance 2021: OECD Indicators." OECD Publishing.

https://doi.org/10.1787/b35a14e5-en.

9. Brown, Jennifer. "Colorado abortion rates keep declining. Free IUDs and easier access to the pill are the reason." *The Colorado Sun*. (October 21, 2019).

https://coloradosun.com/2019/10/21/colorado-abortion-rates-keep-declining-free-iuds-and-easier-access-to-the-pill-are-the-reason/.

Chapter 20

1. Lee, Harper. To Kill a Mockingbird. Philadelphia: J.B. Lippencott & Co., 1960, 60.

2. Rohr, Richard. "Fully Human." Center for Action and Contemplation. (May 16, 2016).
https://cac.org/daily-meditations/fully-human-2016-05-16/.

Chapter 21

1. Madgic, Bob. "Trump holds mirror up to America. Do you like what you see?" *Record Searchlight.* (June 16, 2016).

https://archive.redding.com/opinion/speak-your-piece/trump-holds-mirror-up-to-america-do-you-like-what-you-see-34a15fd5-d1e7-0386-e053-0100007ffdae-383173511.html/.

2. Frey, William. "The US will become 'minority white' in 2045, Census projects." Brookings Institute. (March 14, 2018).

https://www.brookings.edu/blog/the-avenue/2018/03/14/the-us-will-become-minority-white-in-2045-census-projects/.

3. Ibid.

Chapter 22

1. Wilson, E.O. "Can Biology Do Better Than Faith?" *NewScientist.com.* (November 2005).

https://www.newscientist.com/article/dn8254-can-biology-do-better-than-faith/.

2. Brooks, Rebecca Beatrice. "The Witchcraft Trial of Margaret Scott." *The History of Massachusetts Blog*. (April 21, 2019).

https://historyofmassachusetts.org/margaret-scott-salem/.

Chapter 23

1. Sagan, Carl. *The Demon Haunted World: Science as a Candle in the Dark*, New York: Ballantine Books, 2011.

2. National Public Radio. "2020 Faith Vote Reflects 2016 Patterns." (November 8, 2020).

https://www.npr.org/2020/11/08/932263516/2020-faith-vote-reflects-2016-patterns.

Chapter 24

1. Dawson, Christopher. *QuotesWave.com*, Accessed July 15, 2022.

https://www.quoteswave.com/text-quotes/100641.

For more information about Daniel Henderson,
or to contact him for speaking engagements,
please visit hendersond.substack.com.

Many voices. One message.

CPSIA information can be obtained
at www.ICGtesting.com
Printed in the USA
JSHW042037251022
32087JS00001B/7

9 781957 007274